The FINISHED Work of CHRIST

Joe McIntyre

THE FINISHED WORK OF CHRIST

Copyright 2020 by Joe McIntyre

Empowering Grace Ministries

Email: empoweringgraceministries@gmail.com

www. EmpoweringGrace.org

The author has capitalized certain words that are not usually capitalized according to standard grammatical practice. This is done for the purpose of clarity and emphasis.

Unless otherwise noted, all Scripture quotations are from the New King James Version of the Bible. Copyright © 1979, 1980, 1982 by Thomas Nelson Inc., publishers. Used by permission.

Other Bible translation copyrights continued at end of book.

ISBN 978-0-9908869-1-4

Printed in the United States of America

OTHER BOOKS BY JOE MCINTYRE

E.W. Kenyon and His Message of Faith

Who We Are in Christ

War Over the Word

Abiding in the Father's Love

Kingdom Warriors

Throne Life

Establishing Our Hearts in the Grace of God

Healing by Faith: Evangelical Christendom's Lost Heritage

The Eternal Defeat of Satan

ACKNOWLEDGEMENTS

I'd like to thank Allison Armerding for her editing and Renée Evans for her pagination. Blessings to you both. Thanks, also, to David Munoz for his great cover design. Finally, to Jim Bryson for pulling it all together.

DEDICATION

I want to dedicate this book to my loving and faithful wife, Pam McIntyre. She has been my support and encouragement for many, many years of ministry. In all the challenges we have faced, she has stood with me and fought at my side. Pam, I find it difficult to imagine life without you. Other than God's redemption in Christ, you are God's greatest gift to me.

CONTENTS

chapter one

WHAT REDEMPTION PROVIDES FOR US

Many believers today know that Christ died for their sins. They have invited Him to be their Savior and trust Him with their eternal destiny. But when it comes to daily living, they continually struggle with their flesh and the influences of the world. Is the gospel powerless in this life? Does it only prepare us for the next? Or has the church failed to understand all that Christ has done for us and the completeness of His provision?

The premise of this book is that God's provision in Christ is "much more" than Satan's work in Adam. Unfortunately, much of the truth of the gospel has been obscured by men's traditions. Jesus said that religious people can be guilty of "making the word of God of no effect through [their] tradition which [they] have handed down" (Mark 7:13).

Sometimes our problem is not that we don't have knowledge, but that the knowledge we have has not come to us by revelation of the Holy Spirit. When Isaiah was rebuking Israel, he said, "Therefore my people have gone into captivity, because they have no knowledge" (Isaiah 5:13). The prophet Hosea echoed this same idea when he said, "My people are destroyed for lack of knowledge" (Hosea 4:6).

THE NEED FOR KNOWLEDGE

Israel was, in matters pertaining to the true God, the most knowledgeable people in the earth. Yet with their unique revelation they failed to live for God and please Him. Men like Abraham, Moses, and David knew God in a different way than the average Israelite. As it says in the 103rd Psalm:

> He made known His ways to Moses, His acts to the children of Israel.
>
> Psalm 103:7

There is a difference between knowing about the acts of God and knowing His ways. Moses had a greater revelation of God than Israel had. For our Christian experience to be life-transforming, we must have a greater revelation of God, not just know about Him.

REVEALED KNOWLEDGE

Our Father calls us to know Him and His Son Jesus in life-transforming ways. Only our Father can reveal His Son to us. Peter experienced the transforming power of divine revelation from the Father:

> When Jesus came into the region of Caesarea Philippi, He asked His disciples, saying, "Who do men say that I, the Son of Man, am?"
>
> So they said, "Some say John the Baptist, some Elijah, and others Jeremiah or one of the prophets."
>
> He said to them, "But who do you say that I am?"
>
> Simon Peter answered and said, "You are the Christ, the Son of the living God."

Jesus answered and said to him, "Blessed are you, Simon Bar-Jonah, *for flesh and blood has not revealed this to you, but My Father who is in heaven.* And I also say to you that you are Peter, and on this rock I will build My church, and the gates of Hades shall not prevail against it. And I will give you the keys of the kingdom of heaven, and whatever you bind on earth will be bound in heaven, and whatever you loose on earth will be loosed in heaven."

Matthew 16:13-19 (my italics)

Notice that when Peter made his bold confession of faith concerning the true identity of Jesus, Jesus immediately recognized that Peter spoke—not from hearsay or speculation—but rather from revelation. We might say Peter's mouth spoke from the abundance of his heart (Mark 12:34). What was in his heart was something the Father had unveiled to him.

We often hear it said that Jesus is the Rock upon which the church is built. But a careful reading of the above passage challenges that assumption. The Rock is Christ revealed by the Father to us. Jesus Himself is the same yesterday, today, and forever (Hebrews 13:8), but the church increases or declines according to its revelation of Jesus. Fresh revelation of Him captures the heart and focuses the life of the individual.

THE NEED FOR REVELATION

The apostle Paul understood the need for progressive revelation of the Father and of the Son's work on our behalf. When he wrote to Ephesus, though they were a church birthed in supernatural demonstration (Acts 19:5- 6, 11), he prayed that they would have "a spirit of wisdom and revelation in the knowledge of Him"—God the Father—and of the greatness of the power demonstrated in the resurrection of Christ (Ephesians 1:17, 19).

Paul's plea to the Father was that He would "flood their hearts with light" (Ephesians 1:18 AMP) and increase their revelation of both the Father's heart and the Son's Finished Work. This prayer (Ephesians 1:15-23) and the prayer in the third chapter of Ephesians (3:14-21), coupled with the prayer in Colossians 1:9-14, make a great prayer to pray for yourself, your loved ones, and your church. (For further teaching on these prayers, my series Praying with Apostolic Authority unfolds their great wealth.)

THE HOLY SPIRIT'S MINISTRY

The apostle Paul lamented the carnality of the Corinthian church and informed them that he was unable to teach them the deeper things about Christ because of it. Speaking with the heart of a father, he explained that he and his fellow ministers in the gospel "speak wisdom among those who are mature" (1 Corinthians 2:6), but not the wisdom of this age:

> But we speak the wisdom of God in a mystery, the hidden wisdom which *God ordained before the ages for our glory,* which none of the rulers of this age knew; for had they known, they would not have crucified the Lord of glory.
>
> But as it is written: "Eye has not seen, nor ear heard, nor have entered into the heart of man the things which God has prepared for those who love Him."
>
> *But God has revealed them to us through His Spirit.* For the Spirit searches all things, yes, the deep things of God. For what man knows the things of a man except the spirit of the man which is in him? Even so no one knows the things of God except the Spirit of God.

Now we have received, not the spirit of the world, but the Spirit who is from God, that we might know the things that have been freely given to us by God.

1 Corinthians 2:7-12

Notice that this hidden wisdom was ordained before the ages for our glory! These hidden riches that the eye has not seen, nor ear heard, nor have entered into the heart of man, are the very things God has prepared for those who love Him, and which we who have received the Holy Spirit can freely know.

Clearly the knowledge Paul is talking about here is revealed knowledge—knowledge that comes to those who love God. As our revelation of the Father and the Son's Finished Work grows, we increase in our love for God, and this draws us into a deepening unveiling of divine things.

In the next chapter, we will consider the proper lens through which to view the Scriptures.

chapter two

CHRIST: THE INTERPRETIVE KEY

The Holy Spirit is the Spirit of revelation. Paul prayed that we might have a spirit of wisdom and revelation in the knowledge of the Father (Ephesians 1:17). Then he prayed that we might understand what is the hope to which the Father has called us (v. 18a), the riches of the glory of the Father's inheritance in us (v. 18b), and the exceeding greatness of His power working in us (v. 19)—in accordance with the power that raised Christ from the dead.

The Father demonstrated His love and power through what He accomplished in Christ. So how does our revelation of Christ increase? In this chapter, I want us to examine a key to understanding and growing in the revelation of Christ.

Scholars of the New Testament are often surprised by the way the writers of the New Testament use Old Testament Scriptures. In Matthew's Gospel, for example, he describes Joseph, Mary, and Jesus leaving Egypt and quotes Hosea 11:1: "Out of Egypt I called My Son" (Matthew 2:15). But when we read the whole verse in Hosea, it says, "When Israel was a child, I loved him; and out of Egypt I called My son." In its Old Testament setting, this verse is clearly talking about natural Israel.

God originally stated that Israel was His son in Exodus 4:22: "Israel is My son, My firstborn." Yet Matthew, under the inspiration of the Holy Spirit, uses Hosea 11:1 to show that it was prophesied that Jesus would be brought out of Egypt! How can this be?

THE BIBLE IS ABOUT CHRIST

When some of Christ's disciples were on their way to Emmaus after Jesus was crucified, Jesus manifested Himself to them in a veiled form and began talking with them. Their eyes were restrained, so they did not know Him (Luke 24:15-16). In His dialogue with them, He asked them about the things that had happened in Jerusalem in recent days. They said to Him, "The things concerning Jesus of Nazareth, who was a prophet mighty in deed and word before God and all the people" (Luke 24:19).

Jesus responded, "O foolish ones, and slow of heart to believe all the prophets have spoken! Ought not the Christ to have suffered these things and to enter into His glory?" (Luke 24:25-26). The disciples saw Him as a prophet and thought He might be the Messiah, but His death on the cross destroyed their hope of Him actually being the Messiah. Then Jesus did an important thing: "And beginning at Moses and all the prophets, He expounded to them in all the Scriptures the things concerning Himself" (Luke 24:27).

The Scriptures are a revelation of Christ. The history, the teaching, the sacrifices, the feasts—all prophesy of Christ. Woven throughout the stories and the history of Israel are prophetic glimpses of the story of Christ. But it takes the Holy Spirit to unveil Him to our eyes.

THE PROPHETIC ANOINTING REVEALS CHRIST

When the angel spoke to John on the Isle of Patmos, he unveiled this reality that the Scriptures—all written through the spirit of prophecy—are the testimony of Jesus:

> And I fell at his feet to worship him. But he said to me, "See that you do not do that! I am your fellow servant, and of your brethren who have the testimony of Jesus. Worship God! For the testimony of Jesus is the spirit of prophecy."
>
> Revelation 19:10

The spirit of prophecy reveals the testimony of Jesus. The whole Old Testament was written in the spirit of prophecy, so interwoven in it is the testimony of Jesus. Scholars say that there are more references to the Old Testament in the book of Revelation than in any other book of the New Testament. Peter also confirms that the prophets spoke of Jesus—His sufferings and glory:

> Of this salvation the prophets have inquired and searched carefully, who prophesied of the grace that would come to you, searching what, or what manner of time, the Spirit of Christ who was in them was indicating when He testified beforehand the sufferings of Christ and the glories that would follow.

> To them it was revealed that, not to themselves, but to us they were ministering the things which now have been reported to you through those who have preached the gospel to you by the Holy Spirit sent from heaven—things which angels desire to look into.
>
> 1 Peter 1:10-12

Though the prophets didn't know all they were prophesying about, nonetheless they testified beforehand the sufferings of Christ and the glories that would follow.

Remember, when Jesus was talking to the brethren on the road to Emmaus, He said, "Ought not the Christ to have suffered these things and entered into His glory?" These things concerning suffering and glory were present—but hidden—in the Old Testament Scriptures.

THE HOLY SPIRIT LIFTS THE VEIL

It is the Holy Spirit's ministry to unveil Christ to us, as Jesus Himself taught: "But when the Helper comes, whom I shall send to you from the Father, the Spirit of truth who proceeds from the Father, He will testify of Me." (John 15:26). The Holy Spirit, who is the Spirit of prophecy, testifies of Jesus. That is His ministry. He is in us for this purpose.

In 2 Corinthians 3, Paul contrasts the old covenant with the new, explaining that "[God] also made us sufficient as ministers of the new covenant, not of the letter but of the Spirit; for the letter kills, but the Spirit gives life" (2 Corinthians 3:6). He declares the new covenant superior to the old, referring to the old covenant as the ministry of death and condemnation, and the new covenant as a ministry of righteousness and unfading glory (2 Corinthians 3:7-10).

Paul then speaks of Moses—the mediator of the law— coming down out of the presence of God and having to put a veil over his face because of the glory he reflected. That glory, he says, was a fading glory, like the glory of the old covenant. He goes on to say that Israel has a veil over their eyes when they read the old covenant Scriptures. They can't see the glory of Christ revealed in the Old Testament. However, that veil is lifted when one is in Christ:

> Nevertheless when one turns to the Lord, the veil is taken away. Now the Lord is the Spirit; and where the Spirit of the Lord is, there is liberty. But we all, with unveiled face, beholding as in a mirror the glory of the Lord, are being transformed into the same image from glory to glory, just as by the Spirit of the Lord.
>
> 2 Corinthians 3:16-18

Reading this verse in its context, the "mirror" in which we behold the glory of the Lord is the Old Testament Scriptures! As we behold Christ with the help of the Holy Spirit in the pages of the Old Testament, the Holy Spirit releases transforming power, and we are changed into the same image that we behold in the Word.

This should encourage us to develop our relationship with the Holy Spirit, who was given to us, "That we might know the things freely given to us by God" (1 Corinthians 1:14). The Bible is about Christ. As He is revealed to us, our lives are transformed.

But we have an enemy who fears we will grow in our revelation of Christ's Finished Work. We will examine this battle in the next chapter.

Chapter three

THE WAR OVER THE WORD

If what I have been saying about the transforming power of a revelation of Christ through the Word is true, then you can understand why there might be some warfare over the Word. In the next chapter of 2 Corinthians, Paul refers to this battle:

> Whose minds the god of this age has blinded, who do not believe, lest the light of the gospel of the glory of Christ, who is the image of God, should shine on them.
>
> 2 Corinthians 4:4

The god of this age seeks to blind minds so that they don't see the glory of Christ. This warfare does not end when we are born again. However, we have experienced a creative work of God within us:

> For it is the God who commanded light to shine out of darkness, who has shone in our hearts to give the light of the knowledge of the glory of God in the face of Jesus Christ.
>
> 2 Corinthians 4:6

In a prophetic fulfillment of the type of the physical creation, God once again said, "Light, be!" and a new creation came forth within us. We have beheld, in a measure, the glory of Christ, and it resulted in us passing from death to life.

But the war continues over the Word. Jesus taught about it in the parable of the sower:

And He said to them, "Do you not understand this parable? How then will you understand all the parables? The sower sows the word. And these are the ones by the wayside where the word is sown. When they hear, Satan comes immediately and takes away the word that was sown in their hearts."

Mark 4:13-15

Satan greatly fears the revelation of the Word. The Word reveals Christ. When Christ is revealed, lives are transformed and Christ's reality is manifested in the earth. People come to salvation and get healed and delivered. The kingdom advances.

In order for the new creation reality to manifest in our lives, it is necessary that we receive the revelation of Christ in the Word and protect the seed like the good ground: "But the ones that fell on the good ground are those who having heard the word with a noble and good heart, keep it and bear fruit with patience" (Luke 8:15).

Satan greatly fears the Word producing a living faith in us, so he seeks to steal it from our hearts. Jesus tells us that Satan comes immediately to steal the Word that is sown (see Mark 4). He attacks our minds with doubt and fear. He uses the hostility of others and the pressure of circumstances to distract us from the Word. He also uses the anxieties of life, the deceitfulness of riches, and the desire for other things to attempt to steal the Word.

For more on this battle over the Word, see my book *War Over the Word*. This parable is very important to understand.

chapter four

THE IMAGE OF GOD

To really understand what our Father has done for us in Christ, we must see clearly His original intention in creating mankind. Mankind was created for a relationship with our Father through Christ, by which we would function as God's under-rulers.

Because of the effects of sin on our minds, we sometimes find it difficult to grasp that the Father created us for relationship with Himself. So often we are more aware of our sinfulness than we are of the power of the blood to completely cleanse us. A sin-conscious mind hinders the revelation of man's high calling. Man was created as much like the Creator as a created being could be.

OUR CREATED NATURE

The foundational verses about our nature before the fall are Genesis 1:26-28:

> Then God said, "Let Us make man *in Our image*, according to *Our likeness*; let them *have dominion* over the fish of the sea, over the birds of the air, and over the cattle, over all the earth and over every creeping thing that creeps on the earth."

> So God created man in His own image; in the image of God He created him; male and female He created them. Then God blessed them, and God said to them, "Be fruitful and multiply; fill the earth and *subdue it; have dominion* over the fish of the sea, over the birds of the air, and over every living thing that moves on the earth." (my italics)

Our God, as the church has understood Him, is three in one. The Godhead is a perfectly unified fellowship of three personalities in one Being. The point I want to make is that the perfect relationship in the Godhead expresses itself in dominion over all that is created. Mankind was created to enjoy that fellowship and be God's under-ruler. To put it another way, we were to exercise dominion through relationship.

CHRIST, THE IMAGE OF GOD

Because sin captured our minds in unbelief, we soon lost our ability to understand God's purpose and calling in creating us. We lost connection with the One in whose image we were made, and so forgot who we were meant to be. As a result, by the time of the flood, man's mind and heart were overwhelmed with distorted thinking:

> Then the Lord saw that the wickedness of man was great in the earth, and that every intent of the thoughts of his heart was only evil continually. And the Lord was sorry that He had made man on the earth, and He was grieved in His heart.
>
> Genesis 6:5-6

Mankind no longer had any idea of why they were created and the relationship the Father wanted them to enjoy. Their minds and hearts were focused on evil continually. Our Father was grieved in heart by the sin of mankind and the loss of relationship with them.

God wanted us to see what He intended mankind to be like. But all mankind was affected by sin. Even the covenant people were afraid of God. So God's answer was to send His Son into the earth to reveal what "normal" humanity looked like, and to model a healthy relationship with the Father.

Jesus walked as a perfect Human who lived to do His Father's will. While acknowledging the deity of Christ, we also must understand that in His earthly ministry He did not draw upon His deity, but lived as a human anointed by God, and modeled total dependence on God.

Jesus restored the revelation of God to the human race:

> But even if our gospel is veiled, it is veiled to those who are perishing, whose minds the god of this age has blinded, who do not believe, lest the light of the gospel of the glory of Christ, who is the image of God, should shine on them.
>
> 2 Corinthians 4:3-4

Jesus came to show us what "normal" is! The destiny of redeemed mankind is to be conformed to the image of Christ, to be "transformed into the same image from glory to glory, just as by the Spirit of the Lord" (2 Corinthians 3:18).

Paul describes this transformation further in his letter to the Colossians:

> And have put on the new man who is being renewed in knowledge according to the image of Him who created him.
>
> Colossians 3:10

We have put on the new humanity that is being renewed into the image of Him who created him. What was lost in the fall is restored in Christ.

WE WERE CREATED FOR DOMINION

Our Father wanted us to join Him in ruling the universe. He created us for this partnership with Him in subduing creation. Under a prophetic anointing, the psalmist wrote:

> What is man that You are mindful of him, and the son of man that You visit him? For You have made him a little lower than the angels, and You have crowned him with glory and honor. You have made him to have dominion over the works of Your hands; You have put all things under his feet.

> Psalms 8:4-6

In this fascinating description of God's intention for mankind, there is a nugget that many of our translations do not bring out. The original Hebrew word translated "angels" in the fifth verse is Elohim, which is usually translated "God." For this reason, the New American Standard Bible renders it, "Yet You have made him a little lower than God . . ." Young's Literal translation puts it, "And causes him to lack a little of Godhead, And with honour and majesty compasses him." Another version says, "That You have made him little less than divine."[1] These translations enhance our understanding of the psalmist's description of man's high calling.

The New Testament tells us how this high calling has been restored in Christ:

> For He has not put the world to come, of which we speak, in subjection to angels. But one testified in a certain place, saying: "What is man that You are mindful of him, Or the

---

[1] The Writings, A New Translation of the Holy Scriptures. (The Jewish Publication Society of America)

son of man that You take care of him? You have made him a little lower than the angels; You have crowned him with glory and honor, and set him over the works of Your hands. You have put all things in subjection under his feet."

For in that He put all in subjection under him, He left nothing that is not put under him. But now we do not yet see all things put under him. But we see Jesus, who was made a little lower than the angels, for the suffering of death *crowned with glory and honor*, that He, by the grace of God, might taste death for everyone.

For it was fitting for Him, for whom are all things and by whom are all things, in *having brought many sons to glory*, to make the captain of their salvation perfect through sufferings.

Hebrews 2:5- 10 (my italics)

The "world to come" in the above passage is not the next age. The Jewish believers to whom the book of Hebrews was written were living in the forty-year period from Jesus' resurrection to the destruction of Jerusalem and the temple, which completely ended the old covenant and fulfilled what Jesus said would happen at the "end of the age." Once that period ended, the age of Messiah was fully established. In this context, we see Jesus now crowned with the glory and honor intended for mankind. The dominion that was lost to mankind through the fall has been restored to man in Christ.

He, the Firstborn of many brothers and sisters, is the captain of our salvation, and that salvation included the restoration of our authority over the earth. Jesus has won it for us, and now we must enter into this authority.

DOMINION IN HIS NAME

As Jesus' representatives, we have been authorized to go forth in His name and do the works He did:

> Most assuredly, I say to you, he who believes in Me, the works that I do he will do also; and greater works than these he will do, because I go to My Father. And whatever you demand in My name, that I will do, that the Father may be glorified in the Son. If you demand anything in My name, I will do it.
>
> John 14:12-14 MLT

The Father is glorified in the Son when we use the name of Jesus to destroy the works of darkness. We have been authorized to heal the sick and cast out demons so that the Father may be glorified in the Son.

The apostle Paul states this same idea in his letter to the Thessalonians:

> To this end also we pray for you always, that our God will count you worthy of your calling, and fulfill every desire for goodness and the work of faith with power, so that the name of our Lord Jesus will be glorified in you, and you in Him, according to the grace of our God and the Lord Jesus Christ.
>
> 2 Thessalonians 1:11 NASB

CREATED FOR RELATIONSHIP

After Adam sinned, he lost his ability to stand before the face of God. Notice how Young translated this familiar verse:

And they hear the sound of Jehovah God walking up and down in the garden at the breeze of the day, and the man and his wife hide themselves from the face of Jehovah God in the midst of the trees of the garden.

Genesis 3:8 YLT

Sin always brings shame. Adam's and Eve's consciences were flooded with the consciousness of sin. The glory of God, for which they were created, became a terrifying thing. The face of God, with which they apparently had been completely comfortable, now unmasked their sinfulness.

But in looking at what was lost and distorted through sin, we need to realize that the Father had created them to stand before His face without fear or condemnation. He wanted them to walk with Him in fulfilling His unfolding purpose. How it must have grieved the heart of the Father when His children could no longer come and freely fellowship with Him

FAMILY AND COMMUNITY

Sometimes we sing songs that say, "Lord, I don't need anyone but You." While this is in many ways commendable, it does not express God's heart for us. We are created for relationship with God and one another. The community of God—the church—is the expression of the will of the Father. We are created for relationship, through which we rule over creation.

MALE AND FEMALE

God has created us male and female. Both genders are uniquely designed to express the divine nature. We might say mankind has been created for rulership and relationship. Rulership and relationship are in both genders, just in a different balance. Men tend to major on the ruling aspect of the divine nature, while women tend to carry a burden for the relational aspect of the divine. When a man and woman come together in relationship, they become a power tool to release God's dominion. That is one reason why the devil hates the institution of marriage and constantly tries to undermine it.

Single men and women also need to interact in a healthy way with the opposite gender. The genders are complementary. The differences can bring conflict in our fallenness, but godly single men and women need to honor and respect the other gender. When we understand the divine nature as God intended it to reside in us, we can appreciate and respect the differences. Men can call up the dominion in their wife's spirit. Women can draw out a man's need for relationship. In this way, they complete one another. The two become one—fully expressing the divine nature.

Single men and women who understand God's intent can affirm the opposite gender as singles. We honor the uniqueness of the differing genders.

A LIFE ASSIGNMENT

Adam and Eve had an assignment before the fall. They were to exercise dominion in keeping the garden:

> Then the Lord God took the man and put him in the garden of Eden to tend and keep it.
>
> Genesis 2:15

Adam had a job! He had responsibility to tend and keep the garden. He was to reflect the image, likeness, and dominion of God in the garden. He was to rule in the sphere appointed to him by the Father. We, too, are to discover our life assignment and to do it to the glory of God.

We all have a sphere of responsibility in life. We meet with the Father in the "garden," and out of that relationship, we exercise dominion in the sphere of responsibility given to us by Father. This is not a top-down, hierarchical dominion, but a bottom-up, servant dominion.

THE ILLUSION OF INDEPENDENCE

When Satan tempted Eve, he enticed her with the illusion that she could be an independent being. He told her she could know right and wrong independently of God.

It is this deception that has captivated mankind today. People think God wants to take away their freedom! Nothing could be more absurd! As someone once said, "Satan promises us freedom, and makes us slaves. God calls us to be His slaves and sets us free."

The apostle Paul describes this enslaved condition:

> And you He made alive, who were dead in trespasses and sins, in which you once walked according to the course of this world, according to the prince of the power of the air, the spirit who now works in the sons of disobedience, among whom also we all once conducted ourselves in the lusts of our flesh, fulfilling the desires of the flesh and of the mind, and were by nature children of wrath, just as the others.
>
> Ephesians 2:1-3

It is interesting that Paul's phrase "among whom" is translated "in whom" twice earlier in the chapter. In those instances, it is talking about our union with Christ (see 1:11-12). Paul is indicating that our formerly dead and enslaved condition and our new resurrected condition both came about through spiritual union— the first with "the prince of the power of the air," and the second with Christ. We are either in union with Christ or in union with Satan! In the apostle John's first letter, he says, "We know that we are of God, and the whole world lies in the Evil One" (1 John 5:19 TEG). The same language is used to describe our condition before we were saved and after we are saved. Before we were saved, we were in union with Satan. After we are saved, we are in union with Christ.

The being we know as Satan is driven by selfishness. His nature is selfishness. When we live in sin, we are in the grip of selfishness and reflect the nature of Satan. When we come to Christ, our nature is changed so that we can walk in love and forsake our selfish ways.

When Jesus talked about losing our life in order to find it, He was addressing the independent identity we received before we knew God. Our true identity is in Christ. We were chosen in Him before the foundation of the world.

As we perceive the grace of God given to us in Christ before the world began, we let go of the false identity given to us in this world by this world system. Who I am in Christ is my eternal identity. (See my book *Who We Are in Christ*)

TRANSFER OF AUTHORITY

When Adam sinned, the authority given to him by God was transferred to Adam's new lord. The rulership of the earth was usurped by God's enemy. We see this clearly when Satan tempted Jesus:

> Then the devil, taking Him up on a high mountain, showed Him all the kingdoms of the world in a moment of time. And the devil said to Him, "All this authority I will give You, and their glory; for this has been delivered to me, and I give it to whomever I wish. Therefore, if You will worship before me, all will be Yours."
>
> And Jesus answered and said to him, "Get behind Me, Satan! For it is written, 'You shall worship the Lord your God, and Him only you shall serve.'"

Luke 4:5-8

Notice that Satan offered Jesus "All this authority." If Satan did not have this authority to offer, this would not have been a real temptation. Jesus would have said, "You fool. Satan, you do not have this authority to offer." But it was a real temptation because Satan really did have it to offer.

Three times, Jesus referred to Satan as the ruler of this world (see John 12:31; 14:13; 16:11). In the last of these passages, He said that Satan was about to be judged. "Of judgment, because the ruler of this world is judged." In the first of these passages, Jesus speaks of the casting out of Satan that is about to occur:

> Now is the judgment of this world; now the ruler of this world will be cast out.

John 12:31

At the cross, Jesus took all the judgment we deserved and totally paid the price for it. Right before He went to the cross, He spoke to the rulers who were putting Him to death. "When I was with you daily in the temple, you did not try to seize Me. But this is your hour, and the power of darkness" (Luke 22:53). The power of darkness behind the scenes was responsible for the death of Jesus.

JESUS HAS THE KEYS

When the price was fully paid, God the Father raised Him from the dead, overthrowing Satan and stripping him of his deceitfully gained authority. As the RSV translates Colossians 2:15: "He disarmed the principalities and powers and made a public example of them, triumphing over them in him." When God the Father raised Jesus, He made a public example of the principalities and powers of Satan's kingdom. They were stripped of their authority over man and Jesus took the keys of death and Hades (see Revelation 1:18).

Jesus conquered Satan and regained the authority that Adam lost. When He met with His disciples after His resurrection, He said, "All authority has been given to Me in heaven and on earth" (Matthew 28:18). Mankind's lost dominion had been restored through Christ. He gained this authority solely for us. As God, He had no need to regain authority.

In Him we have our dominion restored. In Him, we have been crowned with glory and honor as those set over the works of Father's hands, and we now have dominion.

MUCH MORE

Jesus is God's answer to Adam's transgression. Whenever the apostle Paul compares Adam's sin with Christ's redemption, he always says God's work in Christ is "much more" than Satan's work in Adam (see Romans 5:12-21).

And He did it all for us! Never exalt Satan's work in Adam over God's work in Christ. When you do, you dishonor the tremendous price He paid to redeem us. We dishonor the Finished Work of Christ when we speak of Satan's work in Adam as though it is more effective that God's work in Christ. Glorify God by exalting what He did in Christ!

In the next chapter, we will examine some of the types and shadows of Jesus in the Old Testament.

chapter five

SHADOWS OF REDEMPTION

> For the law, having a shadow of the good things to come,
> and not the very image of the things, can never with these
> same sacrifices, which they offer continually year by year,
> make those who approach perfect.

> Hebrews 10:1

The Old Testament was the apostle Paul's source of confirmation
for the revelation he received from Christ. Illuminated by the
Spirit, he began to see and understand the mystery that had been
hidden for ages, but was now revealed in the light of Christ's
coming. Paul refers to this in Romans 16:

> Now to Him who is able to establish you according to my
> gospel and the preaching of Jesus Christ, according to the
> revelation of the mystery kept secret since the world
> began but now made manifest, and by the prophetic
> Scriptures made known to all nations, according to the
> commandment of the everlasting God, for obedience to
> the faith.

> Romans 16:25-26

Paul shared with his readers that this mystery concerning Christ
is now revealed:

> How that by revelation He made known to me the mystery
> (as I have briefly written already, by which, when you
> read, you may understand my knowledge in the mystery
> of Christ), which in other ages was not made known to the

sons of men, as it has now been revealed by the Spirit to His holy apostles and prophets.

Ephesians 3:3-5

In this chapter, I want to identify just a few of the Old Testament "shadows" that point to Christ. Jesus Himself did just this when He appeared to the men on the road to Emmaus after His resurrection and opened the Scriptures to them: "And beginning at Moses and all the Prophets, He expounded to them in all the Scriptures *the things concerning Himself*" (Luke 24:27, my italics).

CREATION

The Bible begins with the story of creation:

> In the beginning God created the heavens and the earth. The earth was without form, and void; and darkness was on the face of the deep. And the Spirit of God was hovering over the face of the waters. Then God said, "Let there be light"; and there was light.

Genesis 1:1-3

Robert Young suggests we translate that last part of the verse, "Let light be!" God commanded light to come into being.

This foreshadows the new creation in Christ. God commanded His light to shine in our darkness when He revealed His Son to us:

> For it is the God who commanded light to shine out of darkness, who has shone in our hearts to give the light of the knowledge of the glory of God in the face of Jesus Christ.

2 Corinthians 4:6

God's light brought forth a new creation in us! "Therefore, if anyone is in Christ, he is a new creation; old things have passed away; behold, all things have become new"

2 Corinthians 5:17

God's creative ability was expressed in this new creation: "For we are His workmanship, created in Christ Jesus for good works, which God prepared beforehand that we should walk in them" (Ephesians 2:10). Another translation says, "We are God's work of art!" Another says, "His masterpiece."

This world's values and ungodly influences are part of the old creation, and their grip on us is broken. We are no longer defined by this world's appraisal of us. Our identity comes from heaven. For this reason, Paul made this declaration:

> But God forbid that I should boast except in the cross of our Lord Jesus Christ, by whom the world has been crucified to me, and I to the world. For in Christ Jesus neither circumcision nor uncircumcision avails anything, but a new creation.

Galatians 6:14-15

On the cross, Jesus assumed the liability for all we ever did wrong—all our mistakes and poor decisions. He also paid for the healing of anything that was done to us by others. All of those things were dealt with on the cross. We are now part of God's new creation, and the authority of the throne is behind the new creation.

> Then He who sat on the throne said, "Behold, I make all things new." And He said to me, "Write, for these words are true and faithful."

Revelation 21:5

THE BRIDE

After bringing forth creation, God brought forth man. God determined that it was not good for man to be alone (Genesis 2:18). He put Adam to sleep and brought the woman forth out of his side. Looking at her, Adam stated, "'This is now bone of my bone and flesh of my flesh.' Therefore a man shall leave his father and mother and they shall become one flesh" (Genesis 2:23-24).

Before he sinned, Adam prophesied the institution of marriage. He foresaw future generations, how they would reproduce, and how a mother and father would give their children in marriage.

In a similar way, the Father brought forth the bride of Christ out of His sleep in death. Paul makes this comparison in Ephesians 5:

> Husbands, love your wives, just as Christ also loved the church and gave Himself for her . . . For we are members of His body, of His flesh and of His bones "For this reason a man shall leave his father and mother and be joined to his wife, and the two shall become one flesh." This is a great mystery, but I speak concerning Christ and the church.
>
> Ephesians 5:25, 30-32

Paul draws his imagery for understanding the church from the Genesis account of the creation of the woman.

THE DAY OF ATONEMENT

Another Old Testament picture that unveils an aspect of Christ's Finished Work is the Day of Atonement. On this day, the high priest took blood behind the second veil of the tabernacle and sprinkled it on the mercy seat, where the presence of God manifested (Leviticus 16:2).

The priest was instructed to bring two goats and cast lots to decide which was the sin offering and which was to make atonement (Leviticus 16:8-10). The goat that was the sin offering was slain and its blood sprinkled on the mercy seat.

The high priest laid his hands on the other goat and confessed the iniquities of the people over it, "putting them on the head of the goat . . . [and] the goat shall bear on itself all their iniquities . . ." (Leviticus 16:21-22). Compare that with Isaiah 53:6: "All we like sheep have gone astray; we have turned, every one, to his own way; and the Lord has laid on Him the iniquity of us all."

The picture is quite a clear foreshadowing of what Christ did for us. He fulfilled the shadow of both goats. His blood was shed and taken behind the veil and sprinkled on the heavenly mercy seat:

> Not with the blood of goats and calves, but with His own blood He entered the Most Holy Place once for all, having obtained eternal redemption.
>
> For if the blood of bulls and goats and the ashes of a heifer, sprinkling the unclean, sanctifies for the purifying of the flesh, how much more shall the blood of Christ, who through the eternal Spirit offered Himself without spot to God, cleanse your conscience from dead works to serve the living God?
>
> And for this reason He is the Mediator of the new covenant, by means of death, for the redemption of the transgressions under the first covenant, that those who are called may receive the promise of the eternal inheritance.
>
> Hebrews 9:12-15

Later in that same chapter we read:

> For Christ has not entered the holy places made with hands, which are copies of the true, but into heaven itself, now to appear in the presence of God for us; not that He should offer Himself often, as the high priest enters the Most Holy Place every year with blood of another—He then would have had to suffer often since the foundation of the world; but now, once at the end of the ages, He has appeared to put away sin by the sacrifice of Himself.
>
> Hebrews 9:24-26

In the Old Testament, the sacrifice was called "atonement," which means "to cover." The best the Old Testament sacrifices could do was to cover sin.

The only time the word "atonement" is used in the New Testament is in Romans 5:11 in the KJV of the Bible: "And not only so, but we also joy in God through our Lord Jesus Christ, by whom we have now received the atonement." The Greek word usually translated "reconciliation" is mistranslated in the KJV as "atonement." Atonement, no matter how popular a word with theologians, is not a New Testament word!

Why is this important to note? Because the blood of Christ doesn't "cover" our sins; it takes them away! Jesus' blood cleanses us completely and provides for a new creation to be brought forth in our recreated human spirits. Behold! All things have become new!

THE PASSOVER

Another Old Testament type of Christ's work is the Passover, which is described in Exodus 12. A lamb without blemish was to be slain and the blood of the lamb put on the doorpost and lintel of the house. They were then to eat the flesh of the lamb. The blood protected them from the death angel. Eating the flesh provided them with supernatural strength for coming out of Egypt:

> He also brought them out with silver and gold, and there was none feeble among His tribes.
>
> Psalm 105:37

An estimated one-million-plus people came out of Egypt and there was not one feeble one among them!

Most believers know about the power of the blood when they take communion, but how many eat the bread (the body of the Lamb) understanding that there is healing in it?

Paul likens the actual unleavened bread used in the Passover celebration to sincerity and truth in the new covenant:

> Therefore purge out the old leaven, that you may be a new lump, since you truly are unleavened. For indeed Christ, our Passover, was sacrificed for us. Therefore let us keep the feast, not with old leaven, nor with the leaven of malice and wickedness, but with the unleavened bread of sincerity and truth.
>
> 1 Corinthians 5:7-8

THE SIGN OF JONAH

Another shadow of redemptive truth is the story of Jonah. As I noted in chapter 2, the prophets ministered as the Spirit of Christ led them. Their words often gave voice to Christ speaking through them. The Spirit of prophecy is the testimony of Jesus. When the

Pharisees wanted Jesus to give them a sign, He pointed them to Jonah:

> Then some of the scribes and Pharisees answered, saying, "Teacher, we want to see a sign from You."

> But He answered and said to them, "An evil and adulterous generation seeks after a sign, and no sign will be given to it except the sign of the prophet Jonah. For as Jonah was three days and three nights in the belly of the great fish, so will the Son of Man be three days and three nights in the heart of the earth."

Matthew 12:38-40

Jesus indicated that the story of Jonah foreshadowed what would happen to Him. In the belly of the fish, Jonah spoke by the Spirit of Christ, saying, "I cried out to the Lord because of my affliction, And He answered me. Out of the belly of Sheol I cried, and You heard my voice" (Jonah 2:2). Jonah was not in Sheol. He was in the belly of the fish! But speaking as a prophet by the Spirit of Christ, he reveals where Jesus was for the three days and three nights He said He would be "in the heart of the earth." (The word translated "belly" is also translated "womb" by a respected Hebrew scholar.)

Notice how this aligns with Peter's quotation of Psalm 16 on the day of Pentecost:

> Men of Israel, hear these words: Jesus of Nazareth, a Man attested by God to you by miracles, wonders, and signs which God did through Him in your midst, as you yourselves also know— Him, being delivered by the determined purpose and foreknowledge of God, you have taken by lawless hands, have crucified, and put to death;

whom God raised up, having loosed the pains of death, because it was not possible that He should be held by it.

For David says concerning Him: "I foresaw the Lord always before my face, for He is at my right hand, that I may not be shaken. Therefore my heart rejoiced, and my tongue was glad; moreover my flesh also will rest in hope. For You will not leave my soul in Hades, nor will You allow Your Holy One to see corruption. You have made known to me the ways of life; You will make me full of joy in Your presence."

Acts 2:22-28

Peter declared that God raised Jesus from the dead, loosening the pains of death. The Greek word translated "pains" is the word for "birth pangs, travail." God did not leave the soul of Jesus in Hades/Sheol; rather it became the womb out of which He was born—born out death into resurrection life.

As Paul says, "And He is the head of the body, the church, who is the beginning, the firstborn out from among the dead, that in all things He may have the preeminence" (Colossians 1:18). Whatever type of Hades we face, our Father can deliver us!

These few examples may serve as an illustration of how the Old Testament Scriptures all reveal Christ and His work on our behalf.

As a result of Adam's sin, our situation required an amazing intervention by the Father. Our Father assumed the responsibility for our sin and sent His Son to deliver us. In the next chapter, we will see how much the Father loved us.

chapter six

THE NEED FOR AN INCARNATION

And the Word became flesh and dwelt among us, and we beheld His glory, the glory as of the only begotten of the Father, full of grace and truth.

John 1:14

The fall resulted in mankind coming under the dominion of Satan. As men called on the name of the Lord, He brought them into relationship with Himself. Though fallen, man was capable of walking with the Lord. But often, men wavered in their loyalty to God and were drawn into the worship of the false gods of the surrounding cultures.

Genesis describes the condition of man shortly before the flood: "Then the Lord saw that the wickedness of man was great in the earth and that every intent of the thoughts of his heart was only evil continually" (Genesis 6:5). Mankind, hopelessly lost in sin and under the dominion of Satan, was totally unable to redeem himself. This situation, of course, did not catch the triune God by surprise. Before time began, God intended to redeem humanity through His Son and the outworking of the plan of redemption (2 Timothy 1:9). But this necessitated an extreme measure—the incarnation.

THE HELPLESSNESS OF THE RACE OF ADAM

Adam's sin had led to death, both spiritual and physical. At the fall, death began its reign:

> Therefore, since the children share in flesh and blood, He Himself likewise also partook of the same, that through death He might render powerless him who had the power of death, that is, the devil, and might free those who through fear of death were subject to slavery all their lives.
>
> Hebrews 2:14-15

Only through God's covenants were men able to escape the dominion of Satan over their lives. Yet they lacked the ability to consistently walk in obedience to God. "For when we were in the flesh, the sinful passions which were aroused by the law were at work in our members to bear fruit to death" (Romans 7:5). The apostle Paul describes the condition of mankind further in his letter to the Ephesians:

> And you He made alive, who were dead in trespasses and sins, in which you once walked according to the course of this world, according to the prince of the power of the air, the spirit who now works in the sons of disobedience, among whom also we all once conducted ourselves in the lusts of our flesh, fulfilling the desires of the flesh and of the mind, and were by nature children of wrath, just as the others.
>
> Ephesians 2:1-3

A little further in this same letter, Paul comments:

> This I say, therefore, and testify in the Lord, that you should no longer walk as the rest of the Gentiles walk, in

the futility of their mind, having their understanding darkened, being alienated from the life of God, because of the ignorance that is in them, because of the blindness of their heart; who, being past feeling, have given themselves over to lewdness, to work all uncleanness with greediness.

Ephesians 4:17-19

Mankind's desperate situation drew the compassion of God in the form of an incarnation. "And the Word became flesh and dwelt among us, and we beheld His glory, the glory as of the only begotten of the Father, full of grace and truth" (John 1:14). This glorious One, whom we know as Jesus, humbled Himself and became a man.

THE HUMANITY OF JESUS

Bible-believing Christians are firmly convinced of the deity of Christ. He was truly God manifested in the flesh. Paul describes how Christ humbled Himself in his letter to the Philippians:

> For, let this mind be in you that [is] also in Christ Jesus, who, being in the form of God, thought [it] not robbery to be equal to God, but did empty himself, the form of a servant having taken, in the likeness of men having been made, and in fashion having been found as a man, he humbled himself, having become obedient unto death— death even of a cross.

Philippians 2: 5-8 YLT

This quite literal translation brings out the amazing humility of the Master as He came to redeem us. Although He was fully deity, He laid aside His powers as deity and really became a man. In our zeal to defend His deity, many in the church have not clearly seen how Jesus limited Himself in His incarnation and lived in dependence on His Father.

While Jesus was truly God manifested in the flesh, we must also understand that He walked and lived while on earth as a human with all the limitations of humanity. For example, Luke's Gospel tells us that He "continued to grow and become strong, increasing in wisdom; and the grace of God was upon Him" (Luke 2:40 NASB). Jesus in His deity did not increase in wisdom. He was all-knowing! But as a limited human, He could grow in wisdom and walk in the grace of His Father.

It is also important to note that He did no miracles until He turned the water into wine after the Holy Spirit came upon Him when He was baptized in the Jordan. "This beginning of signs Jesus did in Cana of Galilee, and manifested His glory; and His disciples believed in Him" (John 2:11).

AN UNFALLEN MAN

It is important to realize that Jesus in His incarnation is the perfect example of an unfallen man! Jesus in His earth walk is a revelation of what Adam was meant to be if he had not fallen. Jesus came as the Last Adam and the Second Man. He took all the sin of the entire Adamic race as the Last Adam, and began a new humanity in His resurrection as the Second Man:

> And so it is written, "The first man Adam became a living soul," The last Adam became a life-giving spirit. However, the spiritual is not first, but the natural, and afterward the spiritual.
>
> The first man was of the earth, made of dust; the Second Man is the Lord from heaven. As was the man of dust, so

also are those who are made of dust; and as is the heavenly Man, so also are those who are heavenly. And as we have borne the image of the man of dust, we shall also bear the image of the heavenly Man.

1 Corinthians 15:45-49

On the cross, Jesus took the judgment due to the Adamic race, and as the Second Man began a new race of redeemed humanity. The price He paid was His own blood: "Therefore take heed to yourselves and to all the flock, among which the Holy Spirit has made you overseers, to shepherd the church of God which He purchased with His own blood" (Acts 20:28).

CHRIST'S UNION WITH US IN OUR SIN

In His incarnation, Jesus became identified with our race. On the cross, He became identified with our sin:

> For He Himself is our peace, who has made both (Jew and Gentile) one, and has broken down the middle wall of separation, having abolished in His flesh the enmity, that is, the law of commandments contained in ordinances, so as to create in Himself one new man from the two, thus making peace, and that He might reconcile them both to God in one body through the cross, thereby putting to death the enmity.

Ephesians 2:14- 16

The law of Moses was crucified with Christ and completely abolished. In the same way Adam's sin affected all his descendants, so Jesus' obedience affects all who put their trust in Him:

For as by one man's disobedience many were made sinners, so also by one Man's obedience many will be made righteous . . . so that as sin reigned in death, even so grace might reign through righteousness to eternal life through Jesus Christ our Lord.

Romans 5:19, 21

The incarnation was necessary because it had to be one of our own race who redeemed us (Hebrews 2:10-12). And now, through our union with Him, we are destined to partake of His glory, both in this life and ultimately in the life to come. The good news is that there is now a Man on the throne who ever lives to intercede for us, and is able to deliver us to the uttermost (Hebrews 7:25).

In the above verse, I pointed to a fact that many in the church have not understood: the law of Moses was crucified with Christ. In the next chapter, we will see that the law fulfilled its purpose and has been laid aside.

chapter seven

THE LAW FULFILLED

One of the great stumbling blocks in our walk with God is trying to live by an outward standard rather than learning to live by a new life imparted within us. Why is this so crucial? Because when mankind tries to live by an external law, we fail to live by the indwelling presence of the Holy Spirit. In this chapter, I will seek to bring clarity on this crucial concept.

THE TWO TREES IN THE GARDEN

The Bible begins with the story of creation and man's place in the garden of Eden. Adam and Eve had but one restriction:

> And the Lord God commanded the man, saying, "Of every tree of the garden you may freely eat; but of the tree of the knowledge of good and evil you shall not eat, for in the day that you eat of it you shall surely die."
>
> Genesis 2:16-17

Notice that the forbidden tree was not just the knowledge of evil. God also forbade them to know the good independently of Himself. In other words, the true knowledge of good and evil was to flow out of Adam and Eve's relationship with God, not by their independent perception of good and evil. They were to walk in and by the Spirit, not by their reasoning faculty or emotions. Satan knew if he could reduce them to dependence on their minds or emotions, he would have no trouble manipulating them to do his will.

Satan seduced them by enticing them toward something good—the knowledge of good and evil—but in a way that would allow him to begin to be their instructor in good and evil, rather than God. Of course, Satan had no intention of instructing them in righteousness, but rather in unrighteousness.

By offering them a way to be independent of God in their quest for knowledge, he seduced them into an unholy dependence on him. They fell from their spirit-to-Spirit relationship with the Father into the dominion of their mind and body over their lives.

A TOTALLY DEPENDENT LIFE

When Jesus came, He modeled a totally dependent life. He only did what He saw His Father doing and only spoke what He heard His Father saying.

He said of Himself that He was meek and lowly in heart, and invited us as His followers to learn of Him and find rest for our souls (Matthew 11:28-30). The root cause of sin in the world is the illusion of and desire for independence. Unbelief is conceived when we see ourselves independent of God.

Jesus is the Tree of Life. As we partake of Him, we are conformed to His image. When the apostle John brought the word of the Lord to the churches in the book of Revelation, he told them that access to the Tree of Life was available to them:

> He who has an ear, let him hear what the Spirit says to the churches. To him who overcomes I will give to eat from the tree of life, which is in the midst of the Paradise of God.
>
> Revelation 2:7

As we cultivate our relationship with the Father through Jesus, we become partakers of the Tree of Life. What Adam lost, Jesus has restored.

THE LAW CRUCIFIED

Man in his fallenness no longer felt at home in the presence of Father God. The more mankind withdrew from God, the more deceived they became. To remedy this situation, God began to make covenants with various individuals. Eventually, he called Abraham into a covenant and promised to bless the nations through his seed.

To further separate Abraham's descendants from the pagan nations around them, he gave them a law and a sacrificial system. God knew that mankind could not keep the law. He gave it to reveal to man his need of a Savior. The sacrificial system pointed to Christ. The law showed them their need for a substitute:

> For no person will be justified (made righteous, acquitted, and judged acceptable) in His sight by observing the works prescribed by the Law. For [the real function of] the Law is to make men recognize and be conscious of sin [not mere perception, but an acquaintance with sin which works toward repentance, faith, and holy character].

> Romans 3:20 AMP

The purpose of the law was to make men conscious of their sin. God knew they couldn't keep the law. It was designed to show men their need.

Humanity was so deep in darkness that they really thought they could do whatever God asked them to do. Father needed to show them how their thinking was misguided. Notice what Paul says in his letter to the Corinthians:

> But if *the ministry of death*, written and engraved on stones, was glorious, so that the children of Israel could not look steadily at the face of Moses because of the glory of his countenance, which glory was *passing away*, how will the ministry of the Spirit not be more glorious? For if *the ministry of condemnation* had glory, the ministry of righteousness exceeds much more in glory. For even what was made glorious had no glory in this respect, because of the glory that excels. For if what is passing away was glorious, what remains is much more glorious.
>
> 2 Corinthians 3:7-11 (my italics)

Notice how Paul describes the law: "the ministry of death and condemnation." In the Greek of the New Testament, Paul uses a word that we translate "passing away," but which means "to make ineffective, destroy, render powerless, annul."

The law of Moses, including the Ten Commandments, is no longer the governing standard for the Christian. Don't get nervous! I will explain what I mean as we proceed. But I did make the clear observation that Paul tells us that the law—including the Ten Commandments—was crucified with Christ.

> Having wiped out the handwriting of requirements that was against us, which was contrary to us. And He has taken it out of the way, having nailed it to the cross.
>
> Colossians 2:14

This refers to the whole law, but specifically to the Ten Commandments. Paul tells us that it is the law that empowered sin: "The sting of death is sin, and the strength of sin is the law" (1 Corinthians 15:56).

The word translated "strength" in this passage is *dunamis*. This is the word used to describe supernatural power throughout the New Testament. It is the "thou shalt nots" of the law that reveal our sinfulness. As Paul said in Romans 7:

> What shall we say then? Is the law sin? Certainly not! On the contrary, I would not have known sin except through the law. For I would not have known covetousness unless the law had said, "You shall not covet."
>
> Romans 7:7

So the law actually empowers and reveals sin. "Therefore, my brethren, you also have died to the law through the body of Christ, that you may be married to another—to Him who was raised from the dead, that we should bear fruit to God" (v. 4). Now through our union with Christ, we find the ability to bring forth fruit that pleases God:

> For on the one hand there is an annulling of the former commandment because of its weakness and unprofitableness, for the law made nothing perfect; on the other hand, there is the bringing in of a better hope, through which we draw near to God.
>
> Hebrews 7:18-19

Christ, our better hope, enables us to draw near to God without condemnation, so that we might receive God's enabling grace to live a life pleasing to Him. Paul describes the way in which the Father solved the dilemma of the Jews under the law and the Gentiles without the law:

For He Himself is our peace, who has made both (Jew and Gentile) one, and has broken down the middle wall of separation, having abolished in His flesh the enmity, that is, *the law of commandments contained in ordinances*, so as to create in Himself one new man from the two, thus making peace, and that He might reconcile them both to God in one body through the cross, thereby putting to death the enmity.

Ephesians 2:14-16 (my italics)

Again, we see that the law was abolished on the cross. The entire Adamic race, Jew and Gentile, was reconciled to God through the cross in one body: the body of Christ.

As part of God's one new man—Christ, Head and body— we are free from the burden of legalistic living. Christ, our righteousness, is living in us now, and as we learn to draw upon His indwelling presence, we fulfill the righteous requirement of the law:

Owe no one anything except to love one another, for he who loves another has fulfilled the law. For the commandments, "You shall not commit adultery," "You shall not murder," "You shall not steal," "You shall not bear false witness," "You shall not covet," and if there is any other commandment, are all summed up in this saying, namely, "You shall love your neighbor as yourself." Love does no harm to a neighbor; therefore love is the fulfillment of the law.

Romans 13:8-10

Paul had discovered that Christ lived in him (Galatians 2:20). He longed for those to whom he ministered to grasp this profound reality: "My little children, for whom I labor in birth again until Christ is formed in you" (Galatians 4:19). Because of this reality, we must no longer try to obtain righteousness through the law, but instead should recognize that Christ has fulfilled the law and freed us to walk in His righteousness by following the Spirit:

> There is therefore now no condemnation to those who are in Christ Jesus, who do not walk according to the flesh, but according to the Spirit. For the law of the Spirit of life in Christ Jesus has made me free from the law of sin and death. For what the law could not do in that it was weak through the flesh, God did by sending His own Son in the likeness of sinful flesh, on account of sin: He condemned sin in the flesh, that the righteous requirement of the law might be fulfilled in us who do not walk according to the flesh but according to the Spirit.
>
> Romans 8:1-4

As we learn to yield to the Spirit of God within us, we also will fulfill the righteous requirement of the law— that is, we will love our neighbor as ourselves.

ABRAHAM'S SEED—HEIRS OF GOD

Paul was quite concerned about the Galatians going back to law in their Christian lives. He sought to bring them clarity about the place the law held in God's purposes by reminding them about the nature of covenant. (In the days of the new covenant, all men understood covenant agreements.)

> Brethren, I speak in the manner of men: Though it is only a man's covenant, yet if it is confirmed, no one annuls or adds to it. Now to Abraham and his Seed were the promises made. He does not say, 'And to seeds,' as of many, but as of one, 'And to your Seed,' who is Christ.
>
> Galatians 3:15-16

Here Paul shows us that when God promised to bless Abraham's Seed, He was actually making the promise to Christ:

> And this I say, that the law, which was four hundred and thirty years later, cannot annul the covenant that was confirmed before by God in Christ, that it should make the promise of no effect. For if the inheritance is of the law, it is no longer of promise; but God gave it to Abraham by promise.
>
> Galatians 3:15-18

The promise to Abraham preceded the law by many years:

> What purpose then does the law serve? It was added because of transgressions, till the Seed should come to whom the promise was made; and it was appointed through angels by the hand of a mediator . . . Is the law then against the promises of God? Certainly not! For if there had been a law given which could have given life, truly righteousness would have been by the law.
>
> . . And if you are Christ's, then you are Abraham's seed, and heirs according to the promise.
>
> Galatians 3:15-21, 29

The law brought the knowledge of sin, while the coming of Christ brought the knowledge of righteousness (Romans 1:16, 17). As we grow up in Him, we learn to draw upon the indwelling Holy Spirit and are empowered to walk worthily of the Lord.

Paul comments further on this theme of Abraham's faith bringing him into right standing with God in Romans 4:

> What then shall we say that Abraham our father according to the flesh has found? For if Abraham was justified by works, he has something to boast about, but not before

God. For what does the Scripture say? "Abraham believed God, and it was accounted to him for righteousness." Now to him who works, the wages are not counted as grace but as debt. But to him who does not work but believes on Him who justifies the ungodly, his faith is accounted for righteousness.

Romans 4:1-5

New covenant righteousness is offered on the basis of faith apart from works. As we receive God's grace, we are empowered to obey God. Paul expects to see the Gentile believers who hear the message of grace respond with the obedience that springs from faith:

> Through whom (Jesus) we received divine favor and apostleship to urge among all nations the obedience which faith produces.

Romans 1:5 Blackwelder

He concludes the book of Romans with the same thought:

> Now to Him who is able to establish you in accord with the gospel as I preach it, even the proclamation of Jesus Christ in accord with the disclosure of the mystery which was kept in a state of silence during long ages, but now has been made plain through prophetic Scriptures, [and] by the command of the eternal God, make known to all the Gentiles to bring them to the obedience which faith impels.

Romans 16:25, 26 Blackwelder

In both of the above passages, Paul shows that the result of true faith in the grace of God is active obedience to the will of God.

Grace doesn't mean it doesn't matter how we live, but rather, grace is the empowerment to live a life pleasing to the Father.

What the law could not produce, God by His grace can now produce in us who are believers. The righteous requirement of the law is fulfilled in us who respond to the message of grace and trust in the indwelling presence of the Holy Spirit. As we learn to walk in love, we exhibit the lifestyle God desires. As we partake of the Tree of Life— Christ Himself—we are enabled to fulfill the righteous requirement of the law. All of the sacrifices, feasts, and Sabbaths were done away with.

We grow up into Him in all things, who is the Head, Christ Himself. We grow up in the atmosphere of no condemnation, trusting in the faithfulness of God to bring us to maturity. If we do sin, we have an Advocate with the Father who is the total payment for our sins. If we acknowledge them, He is faithful and righteous to forgive us and cleanse us from all unrighteousness (1 John 1:9-2:2).

On the cross, Jesus took us and all our sinfulness into Himself. We will view how challenging this was for Him in the next chapter.

chapter eight

GETHSEMANE

As we pursue a deeper understanding of the Finished Work of Christ, it is important that we realize the challenge Jesus faced in the garden of Gethsemane. In this chapter, we will examine the deeper aspects of the cup He embraced in obedience to the Father. It was more than physical death that taunted Jesus in the garden. He was contemplating being made sin with our sin.

2 Corinthians 5:21

HIS APPREHENSION

It seems strange to think of Jesus being troubled by anything. Yet in the garden, He is clearly grieved as He contemplates what is before Him:

> Then he said to them, "My soul is overwhelmed with sorrow to the point of death. Stay here and keep watch with me."

> Going a little farther, he fell with his face to the ground and prayed, "My Father, if it is possible, may this cup be taken from me. Yet not as I will, but as you will."

Matthew 26:38-39 NIV

Jesus actually stated that His holy soul was overwhelmed!

As He considered the cup He was being called upon to drink to secure our redemption, it clearly was a great test of His faithfulness to His Father. Hebrews offers a description of this great struggle:

> Who in the days of his flesh, having offered up both supplications and entreaties to him who was able *to save him out of death*, with strong crying and tears; (and having been heard because of his piety).
>
> Hebrews 5:7 Darby (my italics)

In the above more literal translation, it is noted that Jesus was saved out of death, not from death as many translate it. We often speak of the "passion," or suffering, of Christ. His passion began in the garden, and it was there that the victory Christ walked out through the crucifixion was won.

Jesus prayed to His Father in terms of great intimacy and asked if it was possible for Him to fulfill His mission by another way: "And He said, 'Abba, Father, all things are possible for You. Take this cup away from Me; nevertheless, not what I will, but what You will'" (Mark 14:36). The agony of contemplating becoming our sin substitute so exhausted Jesus that an angel came to strengthen Him:

> Saying, "Father, if it is Your will, take this cup away from Me; nevertheless not My will, but Yours, be done." Then an angel appeared to Him from heaven, strengthening Him. And being in agony, He prayed more earnestly. Then His sweat became like great drops of blood falling down to the ground.
>
> Luke 22:42-44

John R. W. Stott comments, "From this contact with human sin his sinless soul recoiled. From the experience of alienation from his Father which the judgment on sin would involve, he hung back in horror."[2] Stott, being a Calvinist, saw Jesus as bearing the wrath of the Father against sin. I see the Father and Son working together to take away Satan's authority so it could be returned to mankind. Satan could no longer accuse us because Jesus took what we deserved.

How we should worship and honor our Lord for being willing to endure such torment to redeem us! Many Bible teachers insist that Jesus became a sin offering, as though He bore our sins on His back like a bag. The apostle Paul said He became sin for us who knew no sin (2 Corinthians 5:21).

A.S. Way's translation of this verse is quite graphic: "Jesus knew not sin; Yet God made Him to be the world's sin for our sakes; That we, whose sin He had thus assumed, might become, by our union with Him, the very righteousness of God."

HIS CUP

The cup that Jesus contemplated was the reality of being abandoned by His Father because of His identification with our sinfulness. C.E.B. Cranfield writes, "The burden of the world's sin, His complete self-identification with sinners, involved not merely a felt, but a real abandonment by His Father."[3]

---

[2] The Cross of Christ, John R. W. Stott, (Downers Grove, IL: Intervarsity Press, 1986), 77.

[3] C.E.B. Cranfield, The Gospel According to St. Mark, The Cambridge Greek Testament Commentary Series, (Cambridge University Press, 1959).

The form and horror of Jesus' death was spoken of in Deuteronomy:

> If a man has committed a sin deserving of death, and he is put to death, and you hang him on a tree, his body shall not remain overnight on the tree, but you shall surely bury him that day, so that you do not defile the land which the Lord your God is giving you as an inheritance; for he who is hanged is accursed of God.
>
> Deuteronomy 21:22- 23

Significantly, when Paul quotes this verse from Deuteronomy in Galatians 3:13, he shortens the quotation: "cursed is everyone who hangs on a tree." Paul doesn't say that God cursed Jesus.

The victory of the cross was won in the garden of Gethsemane! Jesus "counted the cost" to redeem us and chose to pay it for us. He drank the cup we deserved so we can share in the rewards that He received.

Gethsemane was a place of the greatest victory. How we worship our great Savior for His unfailing love! When I first realized this fact of His suffering, it broke me. It was a love beyond imagining! And He did this for all humanity, even while we were in total rebellion. What a gospel!

> Jesus therefore, knowing all the things that were happening to him, went forth, and said to them, "Who are you looking for?"
>
> They answered him, "Jesus of Nazareth." Jesus said to them, "I AM."
>
> Judas also, who betrayed him, was standing with them. When therefore he said to them, "I AM," they went backward, and fell to the ground.

Again therefore he asked them, "Who are you looking for?"

They said, "Jesus of Nazareth."

Jesus answered, "I told you that I AM. If therefore you seek me, let these go their way."

John 18:4-9 WEB

This scene took place after our Lord's great battle to accept the "cup" the Father had asked Him to drink. We see clearly that Jesus had made His decision and won the victory. He was ready to face being abandoned by His Father and sent to Hades.

Satan is no longer able to say that because of our sin, we deserve to be abandoned by God. Jesus received us into Himself on the cross and now we can say, "What I deserved, Jesus took for me. Satan, you have no authority over me whatsoever!"

In the next chapter, we will look at the completeness of His work of redemption on the cross and resurrection.

chapter nine

THE REMEDY OF THE CROSS

We have been laying the groundwork to bring us into the heart of this teaching. We want to understand what God accomplished through His Son's work on the cross and in His resurrection. Derek Prince summarized this work thus: "The sacrifice of Jesus—one perfect, complete, all-sufficient sacrifice that covers the needs of every human being for time and eternity."

Paul said, "But we preach Christ crucified: a stumbling block to Jews and foolishness to Gentiles, but to those whom God has called, both Jews and Greeks, Christ the power of God and the wisdom of God" (1 Corinthians 1:23-24). A key word in understanding this truth is exchange. The cross was the great exchange.

A popular teaching about Christ's work sees Jesus enduring the wrath of God in our place. This idea is inconsistent with many Scriptures. For example:

> For God so loved the world that He gave His only begotten Son, that whoever believes in Him should not perish but have everlasting life. For God did not send His Son into the world to condemn the world, but that the world through Him might be saved.
>
> John 3:16-17

Christ's coming was the expression of God's love for the world, not the appeasement of His anger. This is shown in Paul's comments in 2 Corinthians:

That is, that God was in Christ reconciling the world to Himself, not imputing their trespasses to them, and has committed to us the word of reconciliation. Now then, we are ambassadors for Christ, as though God were pleading through us: we implore you on Christ's behalf, be reconciled to God.

2 Corinthians 5:19-20

When Jesus hung on the cross and said, "Father, forgive them," He was expressing the heart of God toward humanity. That cry was the Father's heart revealed.

The wages of sin is death—becoming subject to the dominion of him who had the power of the death, that is, the devil. Before the cross, Jesus said to the Pharisees, "This is your hour, and the power of darkness" (Luke 22:53). Jesus was going to allow the lord of death to put Him to death. Having no sin of His own, He took our sin and our fallenness upon Himself. It was not the Father's anger, but the law of sin and death—enforced by Satan— that came upon Him on the cross. Satan had tried to kill Jesus many times, and perhaps he was pleasantly surprised that he succeeded (working through the Pharisees and the Romans) in putting Him to death. But the Father allowed it and then raised Jesus (and us) out of the dominion of death and the authority of the devil.

HE TOOK OUR PUNISHMENT THAT WE MIGHT BE FORGIVEN

Most believers are well acquainted with the idea that Christ died for our sins. This is the basic gospel. Paul summarizes the gospel in his letter to the Corinthians:

For what I received I passed on to you as of first importance: that Christ died for our sins according to the

Scriptures, that He was buried, that He was raised on the third day according to the Scriptures.

1 Corinthians 15:3-4

This is what we might call the foundational truth of our redemption. The prophet Isaiah prophesied this hundreds of years before Christ came:

> But He was wounded for our transgressions, He was bruised for our iniquities; The chastisement for our peace was upon Him, and by His stripes we are healed. All we like sheep have gone astray; we have turned, every one, to his own way; And the Lord has laid on Him the iniquity of us all.

Isaiah 53:5-6

In the above verses, the word translated "chastisement" is also translated "punishment." The punishment that our sins deserved came upon our substitute and He bore it. The sin problem is settled. Jesus paid the full price for the sins of humanity. Now all that is necessary is for the unsaved to hear the good news and receive Christ as their Savior.

Through Jesus, we are now reconciled to the Father God. It is not just that we are forgiven; we are brought back into relationship and fellowship with our gracious Father God.

It pleased the Father's heart to bring us back to Himself through His Son's sacrifice. He wanted a father-son (or daughter) relationship with us:

> For it pleased the Father that in Him all the fullness should dwell, and by Him to reconcile all things to Himself, by Him, whether things on earth or things in heaven, having made peace through the blood of His cross. And you, who

once were alienated and enemies in your mind by wicked works, yet now He has reconciled in the body of His flesh through death, to present you holy, and blameless, and above reproach in His sight.

Colossians 1:19-22

By accepting Christ's reconciling work for us, we are presented holy, blameless, and above reproach in His sight!

One of the meanings of the words translated "in His sight" is "before His face." What was lost in the garden, Jesus has won back for us. We can now stand before the Father just like Adam did in the garden before he sinned. Have you dared to believe what grace has done for you?

When we focus on our unworthiness, we deny the glory of His grace. Let it sink in that the Father wanted you in His presence and has opened the way into fellowship with Him. As Paul reports in Ephesians: "In Him we have redemption through His blood, the forgiveness of sins, according to the riches of His grace" (Ephesians 1:7). You are redeemed and above reproach in His sight. It is all by faith, not by your good works.

HE TOOK OUR SIN THAT WE MIGHT HAVE HIS RIGHTEOUSNESS

For I am not ashamed of the Gospel. I see it as the very power of God working for the salvation of everyone who believes it, both Jew and Greek. I see in it God's plan for imparting righteousness to men, a process begun and continued by their faith. For, as the scripture says: 'the just shall live by faith'.

Romans 1:16 Phillips

The good news involves more than forgiveness. In the gospel, there is a revelation of the righteousness of God we receive by faith. The gospel reveals God's plan for imparting righteousness to man. Man's great need was righteousness. The law failed to provide a way to righteousness that would satisfy the heart of God. So God Himself provided a God- satisfying righteousness through our union with Christ: "For He made Him who knew no sin to be sin for us, that we might become the righteousness of God in Him" (2 Corinthians 5:21).

Again, A. S. Way translates this verse quite dramatically:

> Jesus knew no sin; yet God made Him to be the world's sin for our sakes, that we, whose sin He has thus assumed, might become, by our union with Him, the very righteousness of God.

In Christ, we have much more than forgiveness, more than being acquitted. First, we were declared righteous. Then, God recreated us and gave us the gift of righteousness (Romans 5:17), which means being in right standing in covenant with God. He brought us into union with His Son, who is now our righteousness. Perfect right standing with God is a gift of grace.

Have you accepted this amazing gift? Or are you still trying to establish your own righteousness through doing enough good works?

Paul addresses the issue of not receiving God's gift in Romans 10:

> Brothers, my heart's desire and prayer to God for [the Jews] is that they may be saved. I bear them witness that they have a zeal for God, but not according to knowledge. For, being ignorant of the righteousness that comes from God, and seeking to establish their own, they did not

submit to God's righteousness. For Christ is the end of the law for righteousness to everyone who believes.

Romans 10:2-4

J.B. Phillips states this verse wonderfully:

My brothers, from the bottom of my heart I long and pray to God that Israel may be saved! I know from experience what a passion for God they have, but alas, it is not a passion based on knowledge. They do not know God's righteousness, and all the time they are going about trying to prove their own righteousness they have the wrong attitude to receive his. For Christ means the end of the struggle for righteousness-by-the-Law for everyone who believes in him.

Romans 10:1-4

It is possible for us to know, and confidently tell others, that we can only be saved by believing in Jesus and His work on the cross and then turn around and try to grow spiritually by self-effort and striving. This is just what Paul warns about and discourages.

Paul points us to the Father, who has brought us into union with Christ as our righteousness: "But by His doing you are in Christ Jesus, who became to us wisdom from God, and *righteousness*, and sanctification, and redemption." (1 Corinthians 1:30 NASB, my italics). Paul knew the dead end of seeking to establish our own righteousness by our works. Paul spoke of how he wanted to finish his life in regard to righteousness:

Yet indeed I also count all things loss for the excellence of the knowledge of Christ Jesus my Lord, for whom I have suffered the loss of all things, and count them as rubbish, that I may gain Christ and be found in Him, not having my own righteousness, which is from the law, but that which is through faith in Christ, the righteousness which is from God by faith.

Philippians 3:8-9

Paul didn't want to stand before God on the last day and offer Jesus his good works achieved by self-effort. He planned to live in the power of the Holy Spirit and the grace of God, and urged us to follow his example.

HE TOOK OUR SICKNESSES THAT WE MIGHT HAVE HEALING

Many are familiar with God's provision for forgiveness; in fact, more people understand forgiveness than the gift of righteousness. Fewer still have understood that Jesus also paid the price for our healing in His sacrifice. This is clearly brought out in the great redemption chapter of the Bible, Isaiah 53:

> In fact, it was our diseases he bore, our pains from which he suffered; yet we regarded him as punished, stricken and afflicted by God.

Isaiah 53:4-5 CJB

Notice how another translation has it:

> Surely our sicknesses he hath borne, and our pains—he hath carried them, and we—we have esteemed him plagued, smitten of God, and afflicted.

Isaiah 53:4 YLT

And yet another:

> But it was our pain he took, and our diseases were put on him: while to us he seemed as one diseased, on whom God's punishment had come.

Isaiah 53:4 BBE

I have quoted from a number of translations, because many of our modern versions have been translated by scholars who do not want to acknowledge that healing is in Christ's redemptive work. Often they translate the Hebrew words for "pain" and "sicknesses" as "griefs" and "sorrows." But the Holy Spirit gives us His thought in Matthew's Gospel:

> And He cast out the spirits with a word, and healed all who were sick, that it might be fulfilled which was spoken by Isaiah the prophet, saying: "He Himself took our illnesses and bore our sicknesses."
>
> Matthew 8:16-17 ESV

Matthew says that Jesus was fulfilling the Isaiah passage by healing the sick and casting out demons. Peter gives his commentary on the Isaiah passage in his epistle:

> He Himself bore our sins in His own body on the tree, that we, might die to sin, and live to righteousness—by whose wounds you have been healed.
>
> 1 Peter 2:24 ESV

Our salvation is more than forgiveness of sins and a place in heaven when we die. As wonderful as these things are, our Father has purchased far more than that through the sacrifice of His Son. Both the Greek and Hebrew words for "salvation" are much broader than the new birth. Our salvation is instantaneous, progressive, and final when we get a new body. But we can only receive what we see by revelation of the Finished Work of Christ.

HE TOOK OUR DEATH THAT WE MIGHT HAVE HIS LIFE

Spiritual death is separation from God. Physical death is the separation of the spirit and soul from the body. When Paul exhorts the Ephesians not to walk as the Gentile unbelievers, he comments:

> This I say, therefore, and testify in the Lord, that you should no longer walk as the rest of the Gentiles walk, in the futility of their mind, having their understanding darkened, *being alienated from the life of God*, because of the ignorance that is in them, because of the blindness of their heart.
>
> Ephesians 4:17-18 (my italics)

In our lost state, we were alienated from the life of God. This verse tells us that we were created to participate in the life of God and that it is an abnormal state for us to be alienated from God's life. We are told in the book of Hebrews that Jesus broke the dominion of death over us by His sacrifice:

> But we see Jesus, who was made a little lower than the angels, for the suffering of death crowned with glory and honor, that He, by the grace of God, might taste death for everyone. Inasmuch then as the children have partaken of flesh and blood, He Himself likewise shared in the same, that through death He might destroy him who had the power of death, that is, the devil, and release those who through fear of death were all their lifetime subject to bondage.
>
> Hebrews 2:9, 14-15

The fear of death rules the life of most unbelievers, and far too many believers! Jesus has delivered us from the fear of death—both physical and spiritual death. He said, "Most assuredly, I say to you, he who hears My word and believes in Him who sent Me has everlasting life, and shall not come into judgment, but has passed from death into life" (John 5:24).

A little later He added, "Most assuredly, I say to you, if anyone keeps My word he shall never see death" (John 8:51). Notice in the above passage that to receive life is to not come into judgment. No condemnation in Christ!

Jesus has broken the dominion of death and released us from the fear of death. Though our bodies will die if the Lord does not return, our inner man will never die. Death's dominion is broken over us.

But there's more! The life into which Jesus promised we would enter is the uncreated life of God. The Father has this life in Himself: "For as the Father has life in Himself, so He has granted the Son to have life in Himself" (John 5:26). This word "life" is the Greek word *zoe*. The Father has *zoe* in Himself and has given to the Son (in His earth walk) to have *zoe* in Himself. Describing His earthly ministry, Jesus said, "I have come that they may have life (*zoe*), and that they may have it more abundantly" (John 10:10).

The life that Jesus came to bring us is the sinless, sickless, deathless life of God! It is the life of the age to come—the age of Messiah's reign, which is now. We receive it in this life and will experience its fullness in the next life. But it is our present possession, and Paul tells us that we are to reign in this life:

> For if, through the transgression of the one individual, Death made use of the one individual to seize the sovereignty, all the more shall those who receive God's overflowing grace and gift of righteousness *reign as kings in Life* through the one individual, Jesus Christ.
>
> Romans 5:17 Weymouth (my italics)

This is the same word *zoe* that describes the life God has in Himself. As our faith grows, we allow this new life to dominate us—renewing and refreshing us— until we fulfill our life's work. We have passed from death into life.

As Paul said, "For the wages of sin is death, but the gift of God is eternal Life in Christ Jesus our Lord" (Romans 6:23). Weymouth gives us, "For the wages paid by Sin are death; but God's free gift is the Life of the Ages bestowed upon us in Christ Jesus our Lord." The Life of the Ages! It is the death-conquering, resurrection life of the Son of God. This is the gift we have received. We have passed from death into indestructible life.

HE TOOK OUR SHAME THAT WE MIGHT HAVE HIS GLORY

Many today wrestle with a sense of shame about their past (or sometimes their present) life. Some feel great shame about what someone else did to them. They can even know they are forgiven, yet still be plagued by a sense of shame. Jesus has paid the price to deliver us from all shame:

> Looking unto Jesus, the author and finisher of our faith, who for the joy that was set before Him endured the cross, *despising* the shame, and has sat down at the right hand of the throne of God.
>
> Hebrews 12:2 (my italics)

When Jesus was made sin with our sin, He took with Him the shame we deserved. On the cross, He experienced the shame of being crucified as the lowest of criminals. As Derek Prince observed in an audio message:

> There is no form of death more shameful than crucifixion. It was the lowest form of punishment for the most debased criminals. They took all of Jesus' clothing away from Him, and He hung naked before the eyes of

the people. Passersby mocked Him. What He endured can be summed up in one word: shame.

Christ endured the shame because He knew that through it, He could bring us to glory.

Hebrews 12:2 in The Passion Translation captures the motivation of Jesus in enduring the shame of the cross quite well: "Because his heart was filled with the joy of knowing that you would be his, he endured the agony of the cross and conquered its humiliation and now sits at the right hand of the throne of God."

The joy set before Jesus, which enabled Him to face the horrible shame of the cross, was seeing, through His eye of faith, the redeemed entering into His glory! "For it was fitting for Him, for whom are all things and by whom are all things (God the Father), in having brought many sons to glory, to make the captain of their salvation (Jesus) perfect through sufferings" (Hebrews 2:10 literal). Out of His tremendous love for us, He took our shame that we might have His glory.

This leads us to the next exchange, which is related to overcoming shame and receiving glory.

HE TOOK OUR REJECTION THAT WE MIGHT HAVE HIS ACCEPTANCE

Jesus endured rejection so that we might be accepted. On the cross, He experienced profound rejection. Isaiah saw it prophetically and spoke of it:

> He is *despised and rejected* by men, a Man of sorrows and acquainted with grief. And we hid, as it were, our faces from Him; He was despised, and we did not esteem Him.
>
> Isaiah 53:3 (my italics)

Even in His earthly ministry, Jesus knew rejection. "He came to His own, and His own did not receive Him" (John 1:11). Jesus was misunderstood even by his own mother and brothers: "I have become a stranger to my brothers, and an alien to my mother's children" (Psalm 69:8).

But Jesus experienced the ultimate rejection when He became identified with us in our sinfulness. He was forsaken by His Father while He was on the cross. This was prophesied hundreds of years before it happened:

> My God, My God, why have You forsaken Me? Why are You so far from helping Me, and from the words of My groaning?
>
> Psalm 22:1

The Gospels record Jesus uttering these words as He hung on the cross:

> And at the ninth hour Jesus cried out with a loud voice, saying, "Eloi, Eloi, lama sabachthani?" which is translated, "My God, My God, why have You forsaken Me?"
>
> Mark 15:34

The Spirit of Christ uttered these words through the prophet long before they fell from the mouth of Jesus. On the cross, Jesus, having taken us and our sin into union with Himself, experienced the rejection of the Father.

In another Messianic psalm, the Spirit of prophecy speaks and describes the sufferings of Jesus:

> Reproach has broken my heart, and I am full of heaviness; I looked for someone to take pity, but there was none; and for comforters, but I found none. They also gave me gall

for my food, and for my thirst they gave me vinegar to drink.

Psalms 69:20-21

The phrase "I am full of heaviness" is literally "I am full of sickness." Jesus not only took our physical sicknesses, but also our mental and emotional pains.

He took the rejection we deserved, so that we could have the complete and total acceptance He deserved: "To the praise of the glory of His grace, by which He made us accepted in the Beloved" (Ephesians 1:6). We are accepted in the Beloved Son of God. Phillips expresses this wonderfully: "That we might learn to praise that glorious generosity of his which has made us welcome in the everlasting love he bears towards the Son."

Interestingly, the phrase translated "made us accepted" is used in only one other place in the New Testament. When Gabriel appeared to Mary, he said, "Rejoice, highly favored one, the Lord is with you; blessed are you among women!" (Luke 1:28). The words "highly favored one" are the same words as "made us accepted" in Ephesians 1:6. Because of what Jesus experienced, we are now highly favored ones!

Because of the breakdown of the family and the missing fathers in our culture, the wound of rejection is rampant. Many find it difficult to see God as Father. The fear of rejection invades the hearts of many believers as they think about approaching the Father.

The good news is Jesus bore our rejection and has made us acceptable to the Father—welcome in the everlasting love of the Father. We can receive it by faith and have the Holy Spirit bear witness with our spirit that we are accepted in the Beloved and are children of God. The Word of truth can set us free from whatever lies the enemy has sown in our lives through rejection. (Sometimes the wound of rejection requires an uprooting of the lie that has gripped the heart. Receiving prayer from those who minister in this area can be helpful.)

HE TOOK OUR CURSE THAT WE MIGHT HAVE HIS BLESSING

Many believers passively accept the curse of the law in their lives because of poor teaching on God's sovereignty. God is surely sovereign, but that does not mean everything that enters our lives is from God. The Bible is clear on issues that our traditions make cloudy. "I call heaven and earth as witnesses today against you, that I have set before you life and death, blessing and cursing; therefore choose life, that both you and your descendants may live" (Deuteronomy 30:19). Life and death, blessing and cursing. Black and white. No gray areas. When we let the Scriptures tell us what is a blessing and what is a curse, it becomes very simple. In Deuteronomy 28:1-14 the blessing of Abraham is outlined:

- Set on high (exalted and honored)
- Fruitfulness and increase
- Health and strength
- Prosperity and success
- Victory over enemies
- The head and not the tail (favor resulting in promotions)
- Above and not beneath (not dominated by anything)

Then the curses are listed in Deuteronomy 28:16-68:

- Humiliated and oppressed
- Lack of fruitfulness and increase
- Every kind of sickness

- Poverty and failure
- Defeat before enemies
- The tail and not the head (disfavor resulting in a lack of promotion)
- Beneath and not above (dominated and subjected)

It is clear what the Bible considers a blessing and what is considered a curse. Jesus bore the curse that we might enjoy the blessing. Some suggest that this was only talking to the Old Testament saints. I cannot find anywhere in the Bible where we are redeemed from the blessing of the law—just the curse! Actually, it wasn't the blessing of the law; it was the blessing of Abraham (see Galatians 3:13).

Paul writes:

> Christ has redeemed us from the curse of the law, having become a curse for us (for it is written, "Cursed is everyone who hangs on a tree"), that *the blessing of Abraham* might come upon the Gentiles in Christ Jesus, that we might receive the promise of the Spirit through faith.
>
> Galatians 3:13-14 (my italics)

As a joint heir with Christ, you have been bequeathed the blessing of Abraham. It is yours by faith and can be claimed once you understand your redemption. You are Abraham's seed and an heir according to the promise (Galatians 3:29).

HE TOOK OUR POVERTY THAT WE MIGHT HAVE HIS ABUNDANCE

This is touched on in our redemption from the curse, but it is clear that Jesus took the poverty curse that we might enjoy abundance.

This means that all of our needs will be met and we will have enough to give to the gospel and minister to the poor and needy. The poverty curse is described in Deuteronomy:

> Moreover all these curses shall come upon you and pursue and overtake you, until you are destroyed, because you did not obey the voice of the Lord your God, to keep His commandments and His statutes which He commanded you.

> Because you did not serve the Lord your God with joy and gladness of heart, for the abundance of everything, therefore you shall serve your enemies, whom the Lord will send against you, in hunger, in thirst, in nakedness, and in need of everything; and He will put a yoke of iron on your neck until He has destroyed you.

> Deuteronomy 28:45, 47-48

On the cross, Jesus was hungry, thirsty, naked, and in want of all things. In His earth walk, He had all His needs met and had a treasurer to hold the overflow, but on the cross, He absorbed the poverty curse.

Paul brings this up in his discourse on finance in 2 Corinthians:

> For you know the grace of our Lord Jesus Christ, that though He was rich, yet for your sakes He became poor, that you through His poverty might become rich.

> 2 Corinthians 8:9

Jesus took the curse and its every effect on spirit, soul, and body, including the poverty curse, that we might enjoy abundance:

And God is able to make all grace abound toward you, that you, always having all sufficiency in all things, may have an abundance for every good work.

2 Corinthians 9:8

The level of God's provision is abundance. As we sow in obedience to God's Word, He promises us a bountiful reaping:

But this I say: He who sows sparingly will also reap sparingly, and he who sows bountifully will also reap bountifully. So let each one give as he purposes in his heart, not grudgingly or of necessity; for God loves a cheerful giver.

2 Corinthians 9:6-7

Christ has redeemed us from the curse of poverty, that the blessing of Abraham might come on the Gentiles through faith. Ask and you will receive.

CONCLUSION

In this chapter, I have attempted to outline some of the amazing riches that have been provided for us in Christ's Finished Work. It is only suggestive. Paul describes the gospel as the unsearchable riches of Christ (see Ephesians 3:8). Let the vision of the tremendous wealth Christ has provided for spirit, soul, and body grip your heart and inspire you to search out what now belongs to you because you are in Christ.

In the next chapter, we look a little deeper into what Jesus endured on the cross: being forsaken by His Father.

chapter ten

FORSAKEN!

Most of us are well aware that Christ died for our sins. But it is possible to see Him as not really entering in to the essence of our lost condition.

Satan, the accuser, undoubtedly insists that we deserved total alienation from God because of our sin. But in God's grace, Jesus swallowed up the rejection and alienation we deserved. When He contemplated the cup He would have to drink, He was overcome with grief at the thought of it!

Many of God's prophets were physically put to death for their faith. We have the record of many in the history of the church who died for their faith and were not the least intimidated by death or the fear of it. So what was it that brought such a feeling of dread on the Son of God? He was contemplating the unthinkable—being alienated from His Father, forsaken in our place! While He was on the cross He expressed this tormenting reality:

> And about the ninth hour Jesus cried out with a loud voice, saying, "Eli, Eli, lama sabachthani?" that is, "My God, My God, why have You forsaken Me?"
>
> Matthew 27:46

Jesus was quoting what the Jews knew as the Twenty-second Psalm. The Bible in Basic English renders the first verse thus:

> My God, my God, why are you turned away from me? Why are you so far from helping me, and from the words of my crying?

On the cross, our Savior experienced alienation from His Father. In the revelation He gave to the apostle Paul, we learn that He embraced the entire Adamic race on the cross, took their alienation into Himself, and was put to death as a result.

In His enduring the crucifixion, Jesus was one with us and came under the dominion of death. Having been forsaken by His Father because of our sin, He experienced not only alienation but physical death and His soul went to Hades. On the day of Pentecost, Peter, under the illumination of the Holy Spirit, quotes Psalm 16 and declares it is a prophecy about Jesus:

> For you will not abandon my soul to Sheol, or let your holy one see corruption. You make known to me the path of life; in your presence there is fullness of joy; at your right hand are pleasures forevermore.

Psalms 16:10-11 ESV

Jesus' soul left His body and went to Hades (or, Sheol). When the Father raised Him (and us in Him) out of death, He re-entered the presence of His Father, or, more literally, He came before the face of His Father, and all the sin of the Adamic race was left behind Him in Hades.

Our past, individually and corporately, was judged, condemned and sent to Hades. When He arose, His ability to come before His Father opened up a new and living way for us to come back into the presence—before the face—of the Father God in Him. Paul tells us we were made alive, raised, and enthroned with Him. (See my book *Throne Life*.)

The way to the Father is opened to us without condemnation. All our deserved alienation was carried by Jesus and we are now accepted in the Beloved Son of God. Welcome, highly favored one!

As I mentioned in chapter 5, Jesus indicated that like Jonah, He would be three days and three nights in the heart of the earth (Matthew 12:40). Although Jonah was in the heart of the great fish, as a prophet he spoke the testimony of Jesus, who was in the belly of Sheol (Hades). The New Heart translation captures this quite well:

> He said, "I called because of my affliction to the LORD. He answered me. Out of the belly of Sheol I cried. You heard my voice."

Jonah 2:2

Notice how the New English Translation expresses Jesus' time in Sheol:

> I went down to the very bottoms of the mountains; The gates of the netherworld barred me in forever; But you brought me up from the Pit, O Lord, my God.

Jonah 2:6

Clearly the spirit of prophecy came upon Jonah and he prophetically gave voice to what our Lord would cry from Hades. He took our place so we could be free. What love this expresses! What grace it releases!

THE OLD HUMANITY

Most of our modern translations give an individual meaning to many of the passages in Paul's letters. For example:

Knowing this, that *our old man* was crucified with Him, that the body of sin might be done away with, that we should no longer be slaves of sin.

Romans 6:6 (my italics)

Many translations say "our old self" instead of "our old man." While these translations capture a truth, I think there is a better way to understand what Paul was saying. Paul is thinking and speaking about humanity in corporate terms:

For as in Adam all die, even so in Christ all shall be made alive.

1 Corinthians 15:22

"In Adam" describes all of humanity, Adam's offspring. Now we who are in Christ are born of Him. He is the head of the new race—a new creation people.

THE GOAL OF REDEMPTION

When the apostle Paul describes what the five ministry gifts will eventually accomplish, he gives this marvelous portrait:

Till we all come to the unity of the faith and of the knowledge of the Son of God, *to a perfect man*, to the measure of the stature of the fullness of Christ . . .

Ephesians 4:13 (my italics)

Who is this "perfect man"? It is Christ—Head and body. God is bringing forth a new humanity who have been called, justified, glorified, and predestined to be conformed to the image of His Son (Romans 8:29-30).

When you begin to think corporately, it opens up many Scriptures to us. When Paul speaks of Christ, he often means the corporate

Christ—Jesus and His body. The entire old humanity in Adam was crucified with Christ and the new humanity in Christ was raised with Him. The Concordant Literal translation of Romans 6:6 captures this:

> knowing this, that our old humanity was crucified together with Him, that the body of Sin may be nullified, for us by no means to be still slaving for Sin.

Paul develops this further in Colossians:

> Do not lie to one another, since *you have put off the old man with his deeds, and have put on the new man* who is renewed in knowledge according to the image of Him who created him, where there is neither Greek nor Jew, circumcised nor uncircumcised, barbarian, Scythian, slave nor free, but Christ is all and in all.
>
> Colossians 3:9-11 (my italics)

You have put off the old man—the old humanity—and are in the process of renewal into knowledge of God's image. What has begun in your spirit is now being worked out in your mind as it is renewed.

Notice Paul says we have—once and for all—put on the new humanity. Some confusion about this comes from what I consider a poor translation of the parallel passage in Ephesians:

> That you put off, concerning your former conduct, the old man which grows corrupt according to the deceitful lusts, and be renewed in the spirit of your mind, and that you put on the new man which was created according to God, in true righteousness and holiness.
>
> Ephesians 4:22-24

This verse sounds like an exhortation to do something— namely, to put off the old humanity. But notice how Greek scholar Kenneth Wuest translates this verse:

> But as for you, not in this manner did you learn *the Christ*, since, indeed, as is the case, you heard and *in Him were taught* just as truth is in Jesus, *that you have put off once for all* with reference to your former manner of life the old man [or humanity] who is being corrupted according to the passionate desires of deceit; moreover, that you are being constantly renewed with reference to the spirit of your mind; and that you have put on once for all the new man [humanity] who after God was created in righteousness and holiness of truth.
>
> Ephesians 4:20 (my italics)

Wuest understands this passage not to be a command to do something, but rather an exhortation to recognize what has already been done for us in Christ, or, as the passage literally says, in the Christ. Now the passage agrees with Colossians.

We are a part of God's new humanity—the new race, the new species. This new creation was created by God out of righteousness and holiness of the truth. Paul, when discussing the new creation, made this observation:

> For the love of Christ compels us, because we judge thus: that if One died for all, then all died; and He died for all, that those who live should live no longer for themselves, but for Him who died for them and rose again.
>
> Therefore, from now on, we regard no one according to the flesh. Even though we have known Christ according to the flesh, yet now we know Him thus no longer. Therefore, if anyone is in Christ, he is a new creation; old things have

passed away; behold, all things have become new. Now all things are of God, who has reconciled us to Himself through Jesus Christ, and has given us the ministry of reconciliation.

2 Corinthians 5:14-18

Because of the revelation Jesus gave him, Paul sees that Christ's death was our death as well. Because of this truth, he says, he no longer views people after the flesh. Seeing what God had provided for lost humanity, he can no longer evaluate them by their sinfulness. He sees them as God intended—part of His new creation. His ministry was to call people to become part of those who are in Christ.

Consider that in the new creation, old things have passed away, all things have become new, and all things are from God. Renewing our minds is coming into agreement with God and the Word that tells us how He sees us. Humility is letting God tell you what the truth is!

Our old life was crucified with Christ. All that we were in the essence of our being was judged and condemned in Him. Now our Father only knows us as who we really are in His Son, not who we were in Adam.

Father knows who you really are. Do you?

chapter eleven

OUR UNION WITH CHRIST

An important aspect of laying hold of our redemption is learning to accept what God says about us in His Word as reality. Next to God Himself, His Word is the highest form of reality. It is unchanging reality—as opposed to this world, which is real, but transitory and subject to change.

Paul says we are already blessed with every spiritual blessing in the heavenly places in Christ (Ephesians 1:3). A better way to translate "heavenly places" would be "the unseen realm of spiritual reality." Father is seeking to teach us to walk by and in these unseen realties. They are completely real, but must be accepted as real by faith.

Many believers want to feel something before they will believe it. Father wants to teach us to walk by realities that we don't always see or feel. We learn to trust Him when He describes spiritual reality. God our Father, who is Spirit, is ultimate reality. We were created to participate in His realm (the garden where the spiritual and the natural meet) and walk in the Spirit with Him. When sin entered, we became dependent on our five senses to discern reality. But God has restored us and called us back to participate in His reality. He describes these realities in His Word, and the life of faith is centered on learning to believe in and rely on these unseen realities. When we do that, God is pleased (see Hebrews 11:6), because this opens the door for Him to be all to us that He desires to be.

When Paul talks about walking in the spirit, we tend to understand that as walking in the Holy Spirit. But there are no capitals or small cases in the original language. So, does he mean that we are to walk in the human spirit, walk in the spirit realm, or walk in the Holy Spirit? I think the best answer is all three!

We are recreated to walk in the spirit realm, governed by our human spirit, and enabled by the Holy Spirit. Father created us as spiritual beings capable of walking in the Spirit. Though Father created us to walk and live in a physical body, the highest part of our being is spiritual. The mind and body are created good as well, but are to be governed by our relationship with the Father in the spirit.

Sin obscured who and what we are in our essence. We are spirit, soul, and body, but our spirit in fellowship with the Father is to be the ruling factor in our lives.

Paul expressed this truth powerfully in 1 Corinthians. He writes, "But he who is joined to the Lord is one spirit" (1 Corinthians 6:17). Our union with Christ in the spirit is so real that he says we are one spirit. Earlier in 1 Corinthians he offers:

> But by His doing you are in Christ Jesus, who became to us wisdom from God, and righteousness and sanctification, and redemption.

> 1 Corinthians 1:30 NASB

The Father placed us in Christ, and now through our union with Him, He wants us to allow Him to be our wisdom, our righteousness, our holiness, and our redemption. Have you ever longed to be righteous or holy? You already are, according to Paul's revelation. Paul is telling us how God sees us. How can two walk together unless they agree?

Because Jesus is now your righteousness, there is no condemnation coming from heaven. When we sin we can grieve the Spirit, but the moment we acknowledge it, we are instantly cleansed of all unrighteousness (1 John 1:9). If you stay focused on yourself after the flesh, you will always wrestle with condemnation. But, with the Spirit's help, you can come to know yourself after the spirit.

When we sin, the Father is grieved because He knows that if we continue to sow to the flesh, we will eventually reap from the flesh. He longs for us not to harvest the corruption sin produces. He is not mad at us, but as a Father, He wants only the best for His children.

He has given us the remedy, whether we sin or just have a need for help: "Let us therefore draw near boldly to the throne of grace that we may obtain mercy and find grace to help in time of need" (Hebrews 4:16).

The word translated "boldness" means "unembarrassed freedom of speech." The only way you can come before the face of the Father with boldness is by believing in Christ's perfect work on your behalf. The blood of Christ cleanses you from all unrighteousness.

IDENTIFICATION

God revealed an amazing truth to the apostle Paul. All the apostles proclaimed that Jesus died for our sins and was raised and enthroned at the Father's right hand. The deeper aspects of Christ's work, however, were unveiled to Paul.

Much wrong teaching has come out of the poor translation of the King James Bible. Two verses in particular have inspired much misunderstanding of Paul:

Knowing this, that our old man *is* crucified with him, that the body of sin might be destroyed, that henceforth we should not serve sin.

Romans 6:6 KJV

I am crucified with Christ: nevertheless I live; yet not I, but Christ liveth in me: and the life which I now live in the flesh I live by the faith of the Son of God, who loved me, and gave himself for me.

Galatians 2:20 KJV (my italics)

These two verses (and a few others) have brought forth a teaching that suggests becoming crucified with Christ is a process of sanctification in which we seek to crucify our "old man" and put "self" to death.

However, these verses do not allow this interpretation. In the Greek of the New Testament, they are "once and for all" acts that God has performed for us, not some grueling process whereby we put ourselves to death.

Two Greek tenses are used in these verses. The Romans passage uses aorist, which in the Greek means "once and for all," and the Galatians passage is in the perfect tense, which means something done in the past with continuing results. These verses speak of what Father has already done for us in Christ, not what we are supposed to make real by "dying out." It is a Finished Work!

But shouldn't we take up our cross, some may ask? Yes, but that doesn't mean a morbid attempt to die to self. It means self-denial and a willingness to be identified with Christ in the world's rejection and the shame of a criminal's death. Jesus was rejected by men and we must be willing to be rejected as those identified with Him.

We do want to renew our minds and bring our bodies into subjection. But we do this as sons and daughters of God who are already completely accepted and have boldness in Christ to receive grace for every challenge and obstacle we face.

As we follow out the revelation God gave to Paul of what Jesus accomplished for us, we find that we have been identified with Him in all that He did. We were crucified, died, and were buried with Him. Then we were made alive with Him, raised with Him, enthroned with Him, and anointed with Him.

After He was enthroned, He received the fullness of anointing as Messiah, which He then poured out on the waiting church in the upper room. What He did, He did for us, not for Himself. All the statements describing His Finished Work are in the perfect or aorist tenses, a once-and-for-all work.

TWO ASPECTS

It is important that we understand the two aspects of new creation life: we are in Christ and Christ is in us. We are once and for all in Christ. But Christ is fully formed in us over time.

Paul referred to this in Galatians: "My little children, for whom I labor in birth again until Christ is formed in you" (Galatians 4:19). The Galatians had been gloriously saved and filled with the Holy Spirit, but then had to contend with people from Jerusalem who failed to understand that the new covenant is about grace working in us by the Spirit and not by being brought into the old covenant by circumcision and law-keeping. Paul wanted them to see that if they learned to cooperate with the indwelling Holy Spirit, He would write the new covenant on their hearts

and enable them to live in a manner that pleases God. Paul was quite passionate about them leaving the law behind and fully embracing and walking in the grace of God! Let Paul's passion take hold of you as well!

chapter twelve

MESSIAH ENTHRONED

One of the sadly underemphasized aspects of Christ's Finished Work is the fact of His enthronement at the Father's right hand. With that under-emphasis is a lack of clear teaching on the fact that we are partakers of His throne.

I once taught through the book of Acts for a Bible school and shocked the students by telling them that nowhere in the book of Acts did they teach, "Christ died for your sins. Ask Him into your heart." No, in the book of Acts they taught that He was taken and crucified, and on the third day He was raised from the dead and is now at the right hand of God. The emphasis was on the conquest of death! Certainly, forgiveness of sins was offered, but in the context of the conquest of death. Take note of Peter's preaching on the day of Pentecost:

> "Men and brethren, let me speak freely to you of the patriarch David, that he is both dead and buried, and his tomb is with us to this day.
>
> Therefore, being a prophet, and knowing that God had sworn with an oath to him that of the fruit of his body, according to the flesh, He would raise up the Christ to sit on his throne, he, foreseeing this, spoke concerning the resurrection of the Christ, that His soul was not left in Hades, nor did His flesh see corruption.
>
> This Jesus God has raised up, of which we are all witnesses. Therefore being exalted to the right hand of God, and having received from the Father the promise of

the Holy Spirit, He poured out this which you now see and hear.

Acts 2:29-33

A few verses later he adds:

For David did not ascend into the heavens, but he says himself: 'The Lord said to my Lord, "Sit at My right hand, till I make Your enemies Your footstool."' Therefore let all the house of Israel know assuredly that God has made this Jesus, whom you crucified, both Lord and Christ."

Acts 2:34-36

Peter had just experienced the arrival of the Holy Spirit. He is preaching under a powerful anointing of the Spirit, who has caused him to see how the truth about the Messiah was woven through the Old Testament Scriptures. The climax of his preaching is Psalm 110, which Israel saw as a Messianic psalm. Peter had heard Jesus refer this psalm to Himself:

He said to them, "How then does David in the Spirit call Him 'Lord,' saying: 'The Lord said to my Lord, "Sit at My right hand, till I make Your enemies Your footstool"'? If David then calls Him 'Lord,' how is He his Son?"

Matthew 22:43-45

Peter realized that this psalm was now fulfilled. Jesus was now sitting at His Father's right hand until all His enemies were under His feet.

We see this good news of the resurrection again emphasized by Peter in Acts 5:

"The God of our fathers raised up Jesus whom you murdered by hanging on a tree. Him God has exalted to His right hand to be

Prince and Savior, to give repentance to Israel and forgiveness of sins. And we are His witnesses to these things, and so also is the Holy Spirit whom God has given to those who obey Him."

Acts 5:30-32

Yes, He died for our sins, but now He is exalted to the right hand of the Father. Forgiveness is now available, and certainly we should preach it, but in the context of Jesus having conquered death and redeemed us from the hand of the one who ruled by the fear of death (see Hebrews 2:14- 15).

The apostle Paul also understood this idea:

> "And we declare to you glad tidings—that promise which was made to the fathers. God has fulfilled this for us their children, in that He has raised up Jesus. As it is also written in the second Psalm:
>
> 'You are My Son,
>
> Today I have begotten You.'
>
> And that He raised Him from the dead, no more to return to corruption, He has spoken thus:
>
> 'I will give you the sure mercies of David.' Therefore He also says in another Psalm:
>
> 'You will not allow Your Holy One to see corruption.'
>
> For David, after he had served his own generation by the will of God, fell asleep, was buried with his fathers, and saw corruption; but He whom God raised up saw no corruption."

Acts 13:32-37

The promised King in the lineage of David has come and now sits upon the throne in heavenly Zion. God proved this by raising Christ from the dead and not allowing His body to see corruption, just as David had prophesied. Sonship, then, came about by the resurrection and enthroning of Jesus. Of course, Jesus was the eternal Son of God, but His human Sonship was declared in His resurrection and enthronement. As Paul notes in the message he preached to the Romans:

He was a descendant of David with respect to his humanity and was declared by the resurrection from the dead to be the powerful Son of God according to the spirit of holiness—Jesus the Messiah, our Lord.

Romans 1:3-5 ISV

Peter and Paul were well aware of what Isaiah prophesied about the seed of David who would come in Israel:

> For unto us a Child is born, unto us a Son is given; and the government will be upon His shoulder. And His name will be called Wonderful, Counselor, Mighty God, Everlasting Father, Prince of Peace. Of the increase of His government and peace there will be no end, upon the throne of David and over His kingdom, to order it and establish it with judgment and justice from that time forward, even forever. The zeal of the Lord of hosts will perform this.

Isaiah 9:6-7

Once the Messiah is seated on the throne of David, of the increase of His government and peace there will be no end. He is seated and His reign has begun. Paul sees Jesus reigning at the right hand of the Father until all His enemies are beneath His feet. He expresses this idea again in 1 Corinthians:

Then comes the end, when he delivers the kingdom to God the Father after destroying every rule and every authority and power. For he must reign until he has put all his enemies under his feet. The last enemy to be destroyed is death. For "God has put all things in subjection under his feet."

1 Corinthians 15:24-27 ESV

This is not what most of us have heard all our lives. These passages show us that Jesus will not deliver the rule of the earth to the Father until He has destroyed every other rule and every authority. The last enemy He will destroy is death. This concept of His present reign being extended is also brought forth in the letter to the Hebrews:

But this man, after offering one sacrifice for sins forever, sat down at the right hand of God. He is now waiting until His enemies are made His footstool. For by one offering He has perfected forever those who are sanctified.

Hebrews 10:12-15 HCSB

We are the body of the enthroned Messiah. He is the Head; we are the body. We have been perfected by His Finished Work. Our minds are being renewed to see, and subsequently, to enter into our authority as His joint-heirs. Jesus has brought many sons (and daughters) to glory.

Another statement that emphasizes this enthronement is in John 7:37-39 CEV:

On the last and most important day of the festival, Jesus stood up and shouted, "If you are thirsty, come to me and drink! Have faith in me, and you will have life-giving water flowing from deep inside you, just as the Scriptures say."

Jesus was talking about the Holy Spirit, who would be given to everyone that had faith in him. The Spirit had not yet been given to anyone, since Jesus had not yet been given his full glory.

The Holy Spirit could not be given as an indwelling presence until Jesus had been given His full glory. On the day of Pentecost, the Holy Spirit was given because Jesus had been given His full glory! His eternal deity is now joined to His perfected humanity. The Man at the right hand of the Father demonstrated His enthronement power by pouring out the Holy Spirit.

The early church, moving in the presence and power of the Holy Spirit, was dynamic proof that Jesus was now seated at the Father's right hand with all authority in heaven and on earth.

In much of the teaching in the church, there is confusion surrounding the varying aspects of Christ's work. In the next chapter, we will look at them.

chapter thirteen

PHASES OF REDEMPTION

It is important to understand the distinctions in varying aspects of Paul's revelation. Many fail to see what we are referring to as the Finished Work. The Finished Work is what the Father accomplished once and for all in His Son, by which He has "blessed us with every spiritual blessing in the unseen realm of spiritual reality in union with Christ" (Ephesians 1:3 MLT).

Many believers are asking God to give them what Paul clearly says is already ours. A good example of this is righteousness. Let me offer Weymouth's translation of Romans 5:17:

> For if, through the transgression of the one individual, death made use of the one individual to seize the sovereignty, all the more shall those who receive God's overflowing grace and gift of righteousness reign as kings in Life through the one individual, Jesus Christ.
>
> In this striking translation, we see that Father has already given us righteousness as a gift! It is the result of His overflowing grace, not any works that we have done or could do. Our part is to believe what Father says and enjoy the gift! Through our union with the Lord in His death, burial, resurrection, and enthronement, we are partakers of the divine nature and joint-heirs with Jesus.

In chapter 9, we considered many aspects of what Christ purchased for us, of which we may now partake. His glory, His righteousness, His healing, His acceptance, His authority, His defeat of Satan, His provision, and many other wonderful benefits now belong to us. As we see them in the Word, we can receive them by faith.

So the Finished Work has to do with what has been done for us. It is a once-and-for-all accomplished work. Nothing can or needs to be added to it.

A MISUNDERSTANDING

One of the statements of Jesus that is often misunderstood is His cry from the cross: "It is finished!" Many sermons have been preached arguing that when Jesus said that, His work was fully accomplished.

But was it?

If we let the book of Hebrews inform us, we see that after Jesus rose from the dead, He brought His own blood into the heavenly Holy of Holies and sprinkled it there:

> But Christ came as High Priest of the good things to come, with the greater and more perfect tabernacle not made with hands, that is, not of this creation. Not with the blood of goats and calves, but with His own blood He entered the Most Holy Place once for all, having obtained eternal redemption.
>
> Hebrews 9:11-12

Jesus' work was not finished until He brought His blood into heaven and sat down at the Father's right hand. Notice this statement: "Now this is the main point of the things we are saying: We have such a High Priest, who is seated at the right hand of the throne of the Majesty in the heavens" (Hebrews 8:1).

So, what was finished on the cross? The law of Moses was finished. Jesus was the final sacrifice that fulfilled all the types and shadows of the Old Testament system. And Jesus' perfect obedience even to the death of the cross was finished (see Philippians 2:5-11). Jesus Himself said to His disciples:

> Behold, we are going up to Jerusalem, and all things that are written by the prophets concerning the Son of Man will be accomplished.

Luke 18:31

The word translated "accomplished" in the above verse is the same word translated "finished "when Jesus was on the cross. All the Old Testament prophecies concerning Jesus would be finished.

On the cross, He commended His spirit into the Father's hand. After three days and three nights, the Father raised Him from the dead. His work was not finished until He presented His blood and sat down at the Father's right hand.

THE PROGRESSIVE WORK

Then there is what God does in us through the Word and the Spirit. This aspect is progressive. No matter what Christ has done for us, it doesn't benefit us until we know about it. Christ dying for us and being raised is finished, once and for all. Christ being formed in us is progressive and ongoing until we are conformed to His image.

So the Spirit, through the ministry of the Word, brings us revelation of the Finished Work. As He does so, it creates faith in us to receive it. The new birth, receiving the Holy Spirit, healing, deliverance, increase, and favor were all purchased for us in Christ's work, but until we gain revelation of them, they do not benefit us.

So the Finished Work is progressively unveiled to us, and as our faith grows, we possess what actually belonged to us the whole time. It is important to learn from the Word what is already ours. When we do this, we often move from petition to declaration. We celebrate what we already have and no longer ask God for it.

If we overemphasize the Finished Work, we can be content with what the Word says even though it is not ours in experience. Paul prayed in many of his letters that these things that are ours would become ours in practical experience by the revelation and empowerment of the Spirit. We are to grow up into Him in all things (Ephesians 4:14).

AT THE FATHER'S RIGHT HAND

A third aspect of redemption that is a great source of encouragement to us is what Jesus is now doing at the right hand of the Father—His present High Priestly ministry.

First of all, Jesus is the Mediator of the new covenant. As He said, "I am the way, the truth, and life. No one comes to the Father except through Me" (John 14:6). We have been saved by means of His heavenly ministry at the right hand of the Father:

> For there is one God and one Mediator between God and men, the Man Christ Jesus, who gave Himself a ransom for all, to be testified in due time.
>
> 1 Timothy 2:5-6

This office is also brought out in Hebrews 8:6:

> But now He has obtained a more excellent ministry, inasmuch as He is also Mediator of a better covenant, which was established on better promises.
>
> Hebrews 8:6

THE CAPTAIN OF OUR SALVATION

According to Hebrews 2:10, Jesus is the captain or Prince- Leader of our salvation:

> For it was fitting for Him, for whom are all things and by whom are all things, in having brought many sons to glory, to make the captain of their salvation perfect through sufferings.

As the captain of our salvation, He has brought us into the glory and honor He now possesses at the right hand of the Father. The word translated "captain" means "originator, founder, leader, chief, first, prince, as distinguished from simply being the cause."[4]

He is the Firstborn of many brothers and sisters (see Romans 8:29). He is also the Firstborn from the dead (Colossians 1:18 Wuest). As we open our hearts to Him, He draws us into sharing His glory at the right hand. This is an important aspect of His heavenly ministry. He is enthroned at the Father's right hand until the Father subjects all things under His feet. He is bringing us to share the glory of this restored authority in our areas of responsibility.

OUR HIGH PRIEST

The letter to the Hebrews strongly emphasizes Jesus as our faithful and merciful High Priest. His king-priest ministry is demonstrated most clearly in the way He shows understanding and compassion toward our weaknesses, for

---

[4] The Complete Word Study Dictionary: New Testament © 1992 by AMG International, Inc. Revised Edition, 1993.

He Himself has faced and overcome weakness:

> Seeing then that we have a great High Priest who has passed through the heavens, Jesus the Son of God, let us hold fast our confession. For we do not have a High Priest who cannot sympathize with our weaknesses, but was in all points tempted as we are, yet without sin. Let us therefore come boldly to the throne of grace that we may obtain mercy and find grace to help in time of need.
>
> Hebrews 4:14-16

As our High Priest, Jesus has made propitiation for our sins (2:17), He is the Apostle and High Priest of our confession (3:1), and He is the reason to hold fast our confession. Our confession is that Jesus, the captain of our salvation has brought us—in this present life—into the glory of the dominion that the Father has given Him.

He sympathizes with our weaknesses, having walked in this world and overcome it. He is our High Priest enthroned at the Father's right hand (8:1). Because of His High Priestly ministry, we have boldness before the Father (10:21-22).

We can hold fast to our confession of faith because we have a sympathetic High Priest at the right hand of God. And because He ever lives to intercede for us, we can have confidence that He will see us through to full salvation.

OUR INTERCESSOR

Jesus' great ministry of intercession was prophesied in Isaiah 53:

> Therefore I will divide Him a portion with the great, and He shall divide the spoil with the strong, because He poured out His soul unto death, and He was numbered

with the transgressors, and He bore the sin of many, and made intercession for the transgressors.

Isaiah 53:12

He was numbered with us, bore our sin, and now makes intercession for us at the right hand of the Father. This is His ongoing ministry on our behalf:

> Therefore He is also able to save to the uttermost those who draw near to God through Him, since *He always lives to make intercession for them.*

Hebrews 7:25 (my italics)

Jesus is always praying for us. And He gets His prayers answered! Father has begun a good work in us and intends to bring us into full or uttermost salvation because Jesus ever lives to intercede for us.

In this wonderful passage in Romans, Paul points to heaven's attitude toward you and me:

> He who did not spare His own Son, but delivered Him up for us all, how shall He not with Him also freely give us all things? Who shall bring charge against God's elect? It is God who justifies. Who is he who condemns? It is Christ who died, and furthermore is also risen, who is even at the right hand of God, who also *makes intercession for us.*

Romans 8:32-34 (my italics)

Heaven is for us—who can be against us? There is no condemnation coming from the Father or the Son. Rather, Jesus is our intercessor and is working to bring the fullness of salvation in our lives. We are being transformed from glory to glory by the Spirit of the Lord, as the veil is lifted off the Scriptures by the Spirit. Jesus is praying for us.

THE SURETY

Another aspect of His heavenly ministry is that of the surety of the new covenant: "By so much more Jesus has become a surety of a better covenant" (Hebrews 7:22). Some translations say "guarantor" instead of surety, which adds to the picture.

A guarantor or surety was a person assuming responsibility for another, as when Judah was a surety for Benjamin:

> I myself will be surety for him; from my hand you shall require him. If I do not bring him back to you and set him before you, then let me bear the blame forever.
>
> Genesis 43:9

Being a surety was being willing to assume the responsibility for another's welfare. As our surety, Jesus has taken full responsibility for our life and well-being, and is the guarantor of our eternal destiny.

OUR FORERUNNER

Jesus opened up the way back into the presence of the Father. He is described as our Forerunner in Hebrews 6:19- 20:

> This hope we have as an anchor of the soul, both sure and steadfast, and which enters the Presence behind the veil, where the forerunner has entered for us, even Jesus, having become High Priest forever according to the order of Melchizedek.

The hope spoken of in this passage is the blessing and multiplication promised to Abraham, as well as sharing dominion with Christ in His present reign. The source of this hope is in the Presence behind the heavenly veil, where our sonship and destiny are confirmed. Jesus not only led the way back into the Father's presence for the rest of the sons and daughters, He became the Way: "I am the Way, the Truth and Life. No one draws near to the Father but by Me" (John 14:6).

In the Sixteenth Psalm, which Peter quoted on the day of Pentecost, we find this statement about our Forerunner:

> For You will not leave my soul in Sheol, nor will You allow Your Holy One to see corruption. You will show me the path of life; in Your presence is fullness of joy; at Your right hand are pleasures forevermore.
>
> Psalms 16:10-11

In this prophetic description of the resurrection and Christ's reentering heaven, we see He was shown the path of life, the way back into the presence of God—the Way to the right hand of the Father.

THE AUTHOR OF OUR SALVATION

The preeminence of Jesus is shown in many ways in the letter to the Hebrews. Another glimpse of His heavenly ministry appears in Hebrews 5:7-9:

> Who, in the days of His flesh, when He had offered up prayers and supplications, with vehement cries and tears to Him who was able to save Him out of death, and was heard because of His godly fear, though He was a Son, yet He learned obedience by the things which He suffered. And having been perfected, He became the *Author of eternal salvation* to all who obey Him. (my italics)

Jesus not only provided our salvation; He Himself is our salvation! In Him we are redeemed and are now partakers of the great salvation which involves us sharing in His dominion (see Hebrews 2:3-9).

THE AUTHOR AND FINISHER OF OUR FAITH

In Hebrews 12, we find another great revelation of Christ's heavenly ministry on our behalf: He is the Author and Finisher (or Perfecter) of our faith. Ever felt weak in faith or in need of stronger faith? Our Lord and Savior is the source and the Perfecter of faith. This is another aspect of His High Priestly ministry. As the Amplified Bible has it:

> Looking away [from all that will distract] to Jesus, Who is the Leader and *the Source of our faith* [giving the first incentive for our belief] and is also *its Finisher* [bringing it to maturity and perfection].
>
> Hebrews 12:2 AMPC (my italics)

At the throne of grace, you and I can find an impartation of grace. Grace received imparts faith. Jesus ever lives to help our faith and save us to the uttermost. Faith isn't something we work up, but is the result of a fresh revelation of His grace.

OUR SHEPHERD

When we think about the Lord our Shepherd, we can be immediately drawn to the Twenty-third Psalm: "The Lord is my shepherd, I shall not want." Certainly, He is our Shepherd. But in the letter to the Hebrews, Jesus is revealed as our Shepherd in a unique aspect of His heavenly ministry:

> Now may the God of peace who brought up our Lord Jesus from the dead, *that great Shepherd of the sheep*, with the blood of the everlasting covenant equip you with all that

is good to do His will, working in us what is pleasing in His sight, through Jesus Christ, to whom be glory forever and ever. Amen.

Hebrews 13:20-21 (my italics)

As our heavenly Shepherd, Jesus has brought us into the new covenant by opening up the new and living way back into the Father's presence through His blood.

As we draw near to the throne of grace, He works in us to enable us to do those things that are well-pleasing in the sight of the Father. He empowers us to do the good works we were foreordained to walk in (see Ephesians 2:10).

OUR ADVOCATE

Another aspect of Jesus' heavenly ministry, which is essential for victorious living, is described in 1 John:

> My little children, these things I write to you, so that you may not sin. And if anyone sins, we have an Advocate with the Father, Jesus Christ the righteous. And He Himself is the propitiation for our sins, and not for ours only but also for the whole world.

1 John 2:1-2

We have an Advocate! When we fail and give place to our flesh, Jesus is always there to intercede and says to the Father, "I already paid for that sin. Do not lay it to their charge." And the Father is faithful and righteous to forgive us and cleanse us from all unrighteousness (1 John 1:9). Forgiveness is always available if we will acknowledge our wrongdoing and ask His forgiveness. We are then cleansed of all unrighteousness!

Instead of an accuser accusing us before God constantly, we now have an Advocate who constantly represents us and pleads our case on the evidence of His shed blood, which has forever silenced the accuser! In the Father's amazing provision in Christ, all we need to do is acknowledge our sin, agreeing with God that we have sinned, and He blots it out as though it had never been.

So in addition to what He has done for us, we also are richly benefited by what He is now doing for us at the Father's right hand.

WHAT HE CAN DO THROUGH US

We have considered His Finished Work—that which is totally accomplished. We have looked at the ongoing work of revelation and empowerment that continues in our lives. And we have seen the many things that Jesus is doing at the right hand of the Father for us. The final aspect of our redemption I want to mention is what the Father can do through us in ministry.

We are all called into the ministry of Christ no matter what our life calling is. The Spirit within us and the Spirit upon us can do the works of Jesus through us:

> And Jesus came and spoke to them, saying, "All authority has been given to Me in heaven and on earth. Go therefore and make disciples of all the nations, baptizing them in the name of the Father and of the Son and of the Holy Spirit, teaching them to observe all things that I have commanded you; and lo, I am with you always, even to the end of the age." Amen.
>
> Matthew 28:18-20

We are to make disciples, baptize them, and teach them to do all things Jesus commanded His disciples to do. Add to that Mark 16:15-18:

> And He said to them, "Go into all the world and preach the gospel to every creature. He who believes and is baptized will be saved; but he who does not believe will be condemned. And these signs will follow those who believe: In My name they will cast out demons; they will speak with new tongues; they will take up serpents; and if they drink anything deadly, it will by no means hurt them; they will lay hands on the sick, and they will recover."

We are also to cast out demons, speak with new tongues, and heal the sick. Notice that these things are for believers to do—not just apostles. The supernatural is to accompany us as we go about our lives. We are to demonstrate kingdom authority as we live our lives.

Jesus said, ". . . the works I do you shall do, and greater works, because I go to the Father" (John 14:12). He went on to say:

> And whatever you demand in My name, that I will do, that the Father may be glorified in the Son. If you demand anything in My name, I will do it.
>
> John 14:13-14 MLT

The word in the above verse usually translated "ask" I have translated literally as "demand." This is not a prayer Scripture. Jesus is talking about doing the works He did. He indicates that we are to do them by using His name. We are not demanding anything from the Father. Rather, we are demanding that the enemy take his hands off the one to whom we are ministering.

It's not about having enough faith. It's about the Father being glorified through many sons and daughters using the name of Jesus to destroy the works of darkness. A little later in John's Gospel, Jesus gives another strong exhortation to use His name to do His works:

> If you abide in Me, and My words abide in you, you will demand what you determine, and it will come into being for you.

> John 15:7 MLT

Again, this is not talking about prayer, but exercising dominion in His name. When we walk in intimate fellowship with the Lord and allow His Word to live in us, we can demand what we determine and it will come into being. Jesus shares His authority and rulership with us. As His joint-heirs, we are being conformed to His image. We are growing up into Him in all things. He is the Firstborn of many brothers and sisters.

As we share the Word and lay hands on the sick, we can expect the Father to honor our obedience to His Word. Every believer can share the good news, pray for the sick, and break demonic oppression off people who are bound.

The Father wants us to know and understand what He has done for us once and for all in Christ. He wants us to cooperate with the ministry of the Holy Spirit through the Word working in us to bring us into our inheritance. Christ is at the right hand of the Father continuing to minister on our behalf, and He wants us to know what He can do through us in ministry as we minister to others.

The Father is bringing all things into subjection under the feet of Jesus.

chapter fourteen

ALL THINGS UNDER HIS FEET

As I noted previously, the modern church has largely overlooked the present reign of Christ enthroned at the right hand of God. Men's traditions have postponed the manifested reign of Christ until after His return.

Bible teachers have also told us that the devil will first take over the planet until Jesus comes and judges him. Most people do not realize that this type of teaching is of recent origin. Only in the last century and a half has the church embraced these ideas. Previously, the church believed that Jesus's reign would extend until the world was dominated by Christian influence.

God says Jesus is now reigning "until" all things are under His feet, while men's traditions say He won't reign "until" His return! Jesus said there is nothing that can render God's Word void except the traditions of men. He said to the religious leaders of His day that they were "making the word of God of no effect through [their] tradition which [you] have handed down" (Mark 7:13).

Paul added this comment about the traditions of men:

> Be careful that you don't let anyone rob you through his philosophy and vain deceit, after the tradition of men, after the elements of the world, and not after Christ.
>
> Colossians 2:8 WEB

In any generation, we may not be aware how much of what we have heard is the traditions of man and not the true Word of God. Well-meaning men without the help of the Spirit have interpreted the Word. Someone has commented that men's interpretations often ascribe to the past what should be for today and delegate to the future that which is for this age.

I think our teachers have done this. What Martin Luther began in the Reformation—dismantling fifteen hundred years of human traditions—is yet incomplete. We are still rediscovering the fullness of the Word. But one thing is for sure: Jesus has all authority in heaven and on earth (Matthew 28:18) and He is now reigning!

In the five hundred years since the Reformation, many realities of the gospel have been restored to the church. In the eighteenth century, during the First Great Awakening, believers discovered that holiness was available. In the latter part of the nineteenth century, they received the revelation of divine healing. In the Pentecostal revivals of the early twentieth century, we learned that the gifts and power of the Holy Spirit are for today. Later in the twentieth century, many found that demonic power could be broken off people's lives. We also discovered that all five ministry gifts—apostles, prophets, evangelists, pastors, and teachers- were for today.

Throughout church history there has always been a remnant walking in these things, but the majority in the church has been ignorant of them. What might yet be left for the church to discover? One of the things that seems to pop up in every generation is the cry, "We've got it all now! The Lord could come any minute."

I'm not so convinced.

HE MUST REIGN

The Word says Jesus will present to Himself a glorious church without spot, wrinkle, or blemish. She will have been washed in the water of Word and be thoroughly sanctified (Ephesians 5:27).

Paul said the five ministry gifts would equip the saints until we all come into the unity of the faith, the full knowledge of the Son of God, unto a perfect man, and reach the measure of stature of the fullness of Christ (Ephesians 4:11-13). In Paul's teaching we see the first man—Adam, the second Man—Christ, and finally, the perfect man—Christ, Head and body! Jesus prayed that the Father would give us His glory so that we might be one as He and the Father are one.

> I do not pray for these alone, but also for those who will believe in Me through their word; that they all may be one, as You, Father, are in Me, and I in You; that they also may be one in Us, that the world may believe that You sent Me. And the glory which You gave Me I have given them, that they may be one just as We are one: I in them, and You in Me; that they may be made perfect in one, and that the world may know that You have sent Me, and have loved them as You have loved Me.
>
> John 17:20-23

The glory the Father gave the Son allowed Him to walk in perfect unity and harmony with His Father while He was on earth. The Father intends us to also walk in this glory— the glory of a shared life with the Father and the Son, one with them in love and in purpose. This union is a union of heart and mind, and through it, the Father intends to convince the world that He sent Jesus!

In our new creation spirit—the part of us that is born from above—we have been perfected. Our spirits partake of the perfection of Christ:

> But this Man, after He had offered one sacrifice for sins forever, sat down at the right hand of God, from that time waiting till His enemies are made His footstool. For by one offering He has perfected forever those who are being sanctified.
>
> Hebrews 10:12-14

By His once-and-for-all offering, He has perfected forever His fellow sons and daughters. Our minds are perhaps in the process of being renewed to these amazing realities, but our spirit has been brought into union with Him and His perfection.

And Jesus is now waiting until all His enemies are made His footstool. He is waiting until the body grows up to be a perfect complement to the Head. Phillip's translates this wonderfully:

> We are not meant to remain as children at the mercy of every chance wind of teaching and the jockeying of men who are expert in the crafty presentation of lies. But we are meant to hold firmly to the truth in love, and to grow up in every way into Christ, the head. For it is from the head that the whole body, as a harmonious structure knit together by the joints with which it is provided, grows by the proper functioning of individual parts to its full maturity in love.
>
> Ephesians 4:14-16

Paul had a clear vision of where the church was headed. We were to grow up in every way into Christ, the Head, who in God's purpose has become a corporate Man—Christ, Head and body.

We, as the body of the reigning Messiah, are to grow up into our place in His current reign. The church is destined to reign. This was His plan for us from before the foundation of the world.

MOVING FORWARD

As I look at the church today, I experience two emotions: one, the clear feeling that we are a long way from the fulfilment of these verses. And two, a sense of rising hope that the Father will perform this Word and fully bring it to pass. The latter thought brings forth in me a longing and a desire to press toward the prize of the upward call of God in Christ Jesus (see Philippians 3:14).

The tremendous amount of division and strife in the various parts of the church testifies loudly that we are not yet walking in the glory the Father and Jesus have given to us. It seems clear that when the body of Christ loves one another as Christ loves us, we might be approaching His return.

This realization should not produce a passive attitude in us, but rather an excitement that there is glory for us straight ahead! Healing and miracles will become increasingly normal in the church. Answered prayer will be the common experience of the saints. The nations will be increasingly discipled and taught the ways of the kingdom. Men and women will go into all walks of life with godly kingdom principles and integrity, and rise to the top of their fields.

Of the increase of His government and peace there will be no end. He must reign until all His enemies are beneath His feet.

The last enemy that will be abolished is death.

BOOKS BY JOE MCINTYRE

E.W. KENYON AND HIS MESSAGE OF FAITH: THE TRUE STORY

Probably few people in modern history have been as unjustly vilified as E.W. Kenyon. This pioneer faith teacher has been accused of bringing metaphysics and other cultish ideas into the church, which in turn, the critics say, influenced the modern faith movement. Is this true? Joe was given access to Kenyon's unpublished works as well as fifty years of his published works to determine the answer. He allows Kenyon, through his writings, to answer his own critics. If you have heard negative things about E.W. Kenyon, get this book. This book will also encourage your faith.

ESTABLISHING OUR HEARTS IN THE GRACE OF GOD

Many believers are unstable in their walk with the Lord because their foundation is not strong. This book points to seven truths that will establish the heart of a believer in the grace of God. Jesus said it wasn't the trials of life that caused shipwreck in a believer's life, but rather the lack of carefully laying our foundation so that the storms of life do not shake us. This book will help you lay a secure foundation that is not overcome by the tests of life.

ABIDING IN THE FATHER'S LOVE

It is impossible to have a healthy faith life if our image of the Father is faulty. The great Father God is perfectly revealed in His Son. This book calls the believer to understand the Father's heart toward His children and learn to receive His love.

THRONE LIFE

In the Apostle Paul's revelation, he shows us things about Christ's Finished Work that we don't see in any of the other New Testament writings. He sees us made alive, raised up and enthroned with Christ, and sharing in His authority. The battle in the earth today is over authority. Jesus has all authority, and He has delegated that authority to His church. Satan greatly fears a church that knows its authority because it will mean his defeat. But it's too late! Paul has shown in his letters what belongs to us and how to enter in. That is the subject of this book.

KINGDOM WARRIORS

This book is a fresh look at the armor of God and what it means in the daily life of a believer who has learned to wear it. Rather than using the Roman soldier as his inspiration, Joe believes that Paul drew his imagery from the Old Testament prophecies of the Messiah in His earthly ministry. We are to clothe, ourselves in this same armor and do the works that Jesus did.

HEALING BY FAITH: Evangelical Christendom's Lost Heritage

In this book, Joe McIntyre looks at the faith teaching espoused by respected Evangelical leaders of the 19th century. They rediscovered the truth of divine healing and were seeing many, many healings. This preceded the Pentecostal movement by many years and the Pentecostals learned healing from these pioneers. This book is a call to follow the example of these leaders in praying for the sick. This book also points to the strong emphasis on faith in God's Word advocated by these leaders and will be an encouragement to any who are looking to the Lord for their own healing.

WHO WE ARE IN CHRIST

The subtitle of this book is Discovering Our Eternal Identity. We were chosen in Christ before the foundation of the world. The Father created you for a relationship with Himself and His Son by joining you in union with Christ. This book unfolds some of the riches that are in our redemption and establishes us in our eternal identity as sons and daughters of God.

WAR OVER THE WORD

In the parable of the sower, Jesus outlines the war over the Word in our lives and how Satan seeks to uproot the Word in our lives before it bears fruit. This study exposes the six things that Satan uses to steal the Word and the graces Father has given to protect the Word so it bears fruit. It is very important for every believer to understand these things.

THE ETERNAL DEFEAT OF SATAN

Many in the body of Christ are waiting for Jesus to return to defeat the devil. They fail to realize He has already accomplished this! When God raised Jesus from the dead, He put Satan to open shame and delivered those who through fear of death were all their lives subject to bondage. Satan greatly fears the church will understand these things and use the authority she already has.

For more by books Joe McIntyre, visit EmpoweringGrace.org to find free video teachings, our blog, and an online store.

ABOUT THE AUTHOR

For more than 35 years, Joe McIntyre's inspired teachings and writings have helped people discover who they are in Christ: loved and welcomed by their Heavenly Father, and able to experience an abundant life in Christ here on earth and throughout eternity. Before going to be with the Lord in 2017, he spent 36 years as founding pastor of Word of His Grace Church, authored nine highly acclaimed books, and traveled the country as a featured speaker. Joe was president of the International Fellowship of Ministries for 12 years, and from 1996 until his passing, served as president of Kenyon's Gospel Publishing Society. Joe's family carries his vision forward today through his 501c3, Empowering Grace, which distributes his teachings and as-yet-unpublished manuscripts.

www.empoweringgrace.org

This book shares some of the treasures
that are already ours in Christ.

For more information by Joe McIntyre, please visit
www.empoweringgrace.org to find free video teachings,
our blog, and an online store.

Made in the USA
Columbia, SC
16 November 2020